ANATOMY

"The bodily structure of waterfowl"

So...... why the Webbed Feet?

Swans, geese and ducks have evolved with webbed feet because those with them were better able to survive than those without them.

Webbed feet are used to paddle & propel through water. For walking on land, they have a raised hind toe to help them stabilise.

The most common type of webbed feet is known as **'palmate'**. This means three toes are completely webbed,

while the fourth hind toe is separate.

Those With
Webbed Feet

All about British Ducks, Geese and Swans

Written and illustrated by

EDWARD GILES

BRAMBLEBY BOOKS

Those with Webbed Feet
All about British Ducks, Geese and Swans

Text and illustrations © Edward Giles, 2017

All rights reserved.
No part of this book may be reproduced in any form, by photocopying or by any electronic or mechanical means, including information, storage or retrieval systems, without permission in writing from both the copyright owner and the publisher of this book.

Edward Giles has asserted his right under the Copyright, Design and Patent Act, 1988, to be identified as author of this book.

ISBN 9781908241573

First reprint in 2018, first published 2017 by Brambleby Books Ltd., UK, in this paperback edition.
www.bramblebybooks.co.uk

Book design by author
Cover design and book layout by Creatix Design
Cover images: front by istock; back by author

Printed and bound by GraphyCems, Spain.

35798642

THOSE WITH
WEBBED FEET

CONTENTS

Acknowledgements	1
Foreword	2
Introduction	4
The Ups and Downs	10
10 Fun Facts	11
The Swans	12
The Geese	26
The Ducks	52
Other Visitors	120
Not One of These?	122
Charities	123
Glossary of 'Fowl Terms'	126
Places to Visit	128
WWT Conservation Work	131
Wetlands of the world	133
Keeping your own Waterfowl	134
Marvels of Migration	142
Index of English Names	144
Index of Latin Names	145

ACKNOWLEDGEMENTS

The success and publication of this book has been considerably enhanced by the input of many experienced 'waterfowlers', for which I am most grateful.

A special thank you to the WWT for their support from the start of this project and provision of a number of images (pp. 58, 63, 75, 87, 108). Also to Jari Peltomäki, an International Awarded Wildlife Photographer, for the kind use of a couple his pictures for the more challenging waterfowl. His photos are on pp. 73, 91, 114.

FOREWORD

For the love of Wildfowl......

"

It does not surprise me that Edward has written a book. From an exceptionally young age he has dedicated himself to this most beloved of hobbies: Wildfowl. The Anatidae or Wildfowl family have captivated enthusiasts for generations; from their appealing behaviours to their stunning beauty, they can simply charm their way into your life. Edward, I believe, is hooked.

Edward was unique amongst young wildfowl enthusiasts in that he was mature enough to seek aid and experience in his childhood collection. It is a rare thing to find a 14-year-old with a pair of Barnacle geese. His desire to diversify and improve made him stand out and as such he made connections with WWT. Here he found aviculturists to aspire to, namely Nigel Jarrett and Mark Roberts, two unique men with decades of experience in species conservation and aviculture under their belts.

As Edward headed away to university and beyond, he found the wildfowl force was still strong, and this love led to running multiple marathons in aid of WWT's endangered species projects. It sets a hearty example to fundraise through extreme physical activity, and after all, where better to see wild birds than in the countryside that surrounds us! I find it truly staggering that Edward has managed to write a book in between his studies and pursuits; if only we could all be so motivated...

His intention of enthusing future generations with a love of wildfowl is most commendable. The Slimbridge Duckery aims to breed and rear endangered wildfowl to educate future generations in the need for Conservation worldwide. It is comforting to know that others share this vision. Books such as this can only help in making the natural world accessible for future generations, and the joy of wildfowl is that there's a species out there for everyone.

For the adventurous there's the South Georgian pintail, a small brown duck that lives so far south towards the Antarctic that they gorge on seal and whale blubber to survive harsh winters. For the designers, there's the Smew and Long-tailed duck, two species so stunning that they look as if they were detailed by a divine calligraphy pen. And who can fail to be moved by two Mute swans inexorably dipping and nodding their graceful long necks to form a romantic white heart?

It really shows a selflessness of spirit that Edward should seek to write such a book, designed to share his love of wildfowl and encourage others to culture an early appreciation for the diverse and astounding array of often unseen birds we are surrounded by in our daily lives. "

Congratulations Edward on an admirable first book.

Phoebe Vaughan
Duckery Warden at WWT Slimbridge
2008 to present

'A little about myself'

There has never been a better time – no matter where you live in the UK – to access the vast number of nature reserves & wildlife attractions up and down the country. As we collectively attempt to move towards a healthier way of living, involving a multitude of lifestyles, bird watching is a great way to become more active and enjoy all the outdoors has to offer.

I was twenty when I started to write this book. I had already been fortunate enough to have built up a private collection of waterfowl over the course of six years at my home in Shropshire. I have been obsessed with all kinds of wildlife since I can remember, but with a particular attraction to birds and even more so waterfowl.

I started off with just a couple of pairs of the native American domestic duck, the Muscovy; popular 'table ducks' and prolific egg layers. However, these only satisfied my interest for a short time as I soon learnt about the many other varieties of ducks through hours engulfed in the work of the great conservationists, naturalists & authors of this field – Sir Peter Scott, Frank Todd and Malcolm Ogilvie, to name but a few.

Muscovy Duck

With the growth of my collection, I have been able to exchange birds with other private collectors, as well as making donations to the Wildfowl & Wetlands Trust, to support the future of both UK & world waterfowl.

Waterfowl have without doubt always been my primary interest. That said, their garden dwelling cousins, the songbirds, have also been a source of inspiration when setting up a hand-crafted nest box business. Throughout school and university, I made various products to sell at country shows, a network of local shops and online. Not only did this provide practical business experience but, more importantly, helped me to fund much of my collection of waterfowl.

So, the main purpose of this book is to introduce waterfowl to enthusiasts of a similar age to when I started, as well as to older generations, perhaps as yet not so experienced in this field. The book embraces the fascinations and fundamentals associated with this family of birds, including, where appropriate, their domestic rearing and aviculture. The design and content are intended to make information easily accessible for the broad spectrum of readers, whilst at the same time revealing and indeed emphasising the amazing characteristics of waterfowl.

My interest in this subject has also involved being a member of leading charities and voluntary organisations in the UK and overseas. The Wildfowl & Wetlands Trust (WWT) has been the one charity I have worked most closely with and actively fundraise for. Other organisations I am a member with include the RSPB, Shropshire Wildlife Trust & the International Wild Waterfowl Association (IWWA), the last of which generously presented me with the award for outstanding achievement by a new aviculturist in 2013.

~ WHAT'S TO KNOW ~

There are **147 species** of ducks, geese and swans found across the world occupying a wide range of habitats. Most typically on public park ponds, as well as meandering reed-lined rivers and choppier coastal habitats where ducks can forage deep underwater for food. Not only do their habitats differ significantly but so do their sizes. The smallest wildfowl in the UK is the Teal — weighing around 250g — in contrast to the migratory Whooper swan which weighs on average around 15kg.

Lamellae

All three families share the similarly webbed feet and flat-shaped bills or beaks that are serrated at the edges by a thin plate-like tissue called lamellae. For swans & geese these act as cutting edges whilst ducks use them as a filtering mechanism to separate nutrients such as small invertebrates and seeds from mud and water.

Most waterfowl also share the tendency of nesting adjacent to some form of water. This provides the best place for rearing offspring due to its safety during and after the nesting period, but also the most readily availability of food. Nests will often be found within the reeds of a river bank, amongst long grass that may surround a large lake or even an island, if available. The last of these is without doubt the safest location in terms of avoiding their most common four-legged terrestrial predator, the fox.

Britain is lucky enough to have **32 species** of wildfowl regularly inhabiting this island over the course of a year. There are, however, a further handful of species – not of British provenance - which either tag along with flocks of other migratory birds or are present in the UK as feral populations, having escaped from captive collections. Some of these 32 species migrate from mainland European countries to breed in the maritime UK climate. A much greater number arrive during the autumn and winter seeking respite from the much harsher weathers in their otherwise native countries. The others are resident here all year round.

~ THE FAMILY ~

The swans are amongst some of the largest flying birds in the world. Featuring their unmistakable long necks and most with wingspans of more than 2 metres, there are seven species across the world, but not all with that well-known crisp white plumage. The UK has four of those species, the Mute – resident here throughout the year – as well as the Bewick's and Whooper swans which arrive from their arctic tundra breeding grounds at the end of September. The Black swan has established a feral population.

Next are the geese of which eight regular species occur in the UK throughout the year; a further five are recognised as rare vagrants. The most common goose in the world is the Greylag, split into the western & eastern races; described as '**polytypic**'.

More terms like this are explained in the glossary on pp.126-127.

The smallest and last members of the waterfowl family are the ducks. There are five principal tribes into which the various species are grouped based on the habitats in which they live, body features and behavioural traits. One of these traits is feeding. Three distinct feeding style preferences occur which are highlighted below.

UP-ENDING
~

This describes the tendency whereby ducks, such as Teal and Shelduck, hoist their rear ends upright in the air to be able to reach below the water's surface for plant matter.

DABBLING
~

When dabbling or surface-feeding, ducks make use of their lamellae as mentioned on p.6. Nutrients such as insects and seeds can be filtered from the mud and water.

DIVING
~

Typical of ducks like Eider and Tufted ducks, this feeding method involves propelling themselves below the water using their larger and further set-back feet.

Domesticated ducks and geese have been important for people's livelihoods for hundreds of years due to their rich eggs & strong-flavoured meat. The wild or ornamental waterfowl have been kept in private collections for aesthetic appeal, commercial breeding exploits and, most importantly, for the critical conservation programs.

~ IUCN ~ → *'The International Union for Conservation of Nature'*

Red List status information is from the 2017 edition of The IUCN Red List.

| LEAST CONCERN | NEAR THREATENED | VULNERABLE | ‹ ENDANGERED › EN | CRITICALLY ENDANGERED | EXTINCT IN THE WILD | EXTINCT |

Species are classified into the above categories on The IUCN Red List of Threatened Species by BirdLife International.

*The status of some species may change in the near future.

~ Family Tree ~

ORDER

ANSERIFORMES
This order encompasses the world's ducks, geese, swans and screamers. Over 140 species are recorded but the exact number is unknown due to uncertainty over some species.

FAMILIES

ANHIMIDAE
Limited to only three South American tropical and sub-tropical birds known as the Screamers

ANATIDAE
The largest family within the order, with worldwide distribution: termed wildfowl in Britain and waterfowl in North America; the ducks, geese and swans

PARANYROCIDAE
A now extinct family, comprising a single known species, restricted to the Miocene of South Dakota

SUB-FAMILIES

ANATINAE - Dabbling ducks
MERGINAE - Sea ducks
AYTHYINAE - Diving ducks
CAIRININAE – Perching ducks
TADORNINAE - Shelduck

ANSERINAE
This sub-family contains the swans and the geese

A further five tribes live across the rest of the world:
* Merganettini – Torrent ducks
* Tachyerinae – Steamer ducks
* Dendrocygninae – Whistling ducks
* Oxyurinae – Stifftail ducks
* Stictonettinae – Freckled ducks

~ KEY OF SYMBOLS ~

Spring/Summer Winter All Year Passage

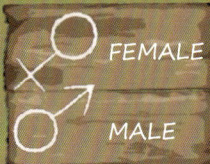

FEMALE
MALE

SMALL MEDIUM LARGE

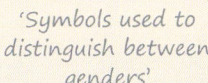

'The primary time of year we can expect to see them'

'Symbols used to distinguish between genders'

'The size of the bird compared to others in their family'

INTRODUCTION | 9

UPs & DOWNs

Since 1999, a report called **'The State of the UK's Birds'** has been produced through the combined efforts of three UK charities, the **WWT**, **RSPB** & **BTO**. The UK's statutory nature conservation bodies, Natural England (NE), Natural Resources Wales (NRW), Scottish Natural Heritage (SNH), the Department of Agriculture, Environment and Rural Affairs - Northern Ireland (DAERA) and the Joint Nature Conservation Committee (JNCC) also contribute significantly to the report. It combines the most recent data from a range of sources to reveal trends about UK-breeding & wintering waterbirds.

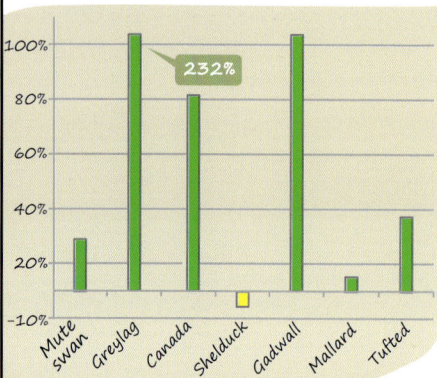

~ BREEDING WATERFOWL ~

2013 saw the first report to cover all UK plants & animals, called the **'State of Nature'**. The information presented in these annual reports relies greatly on the help from thousands of volunteers. They devote much time monitoring the birds and gathering the information needed by the above charities & government agencies to enable the best possible decision making.

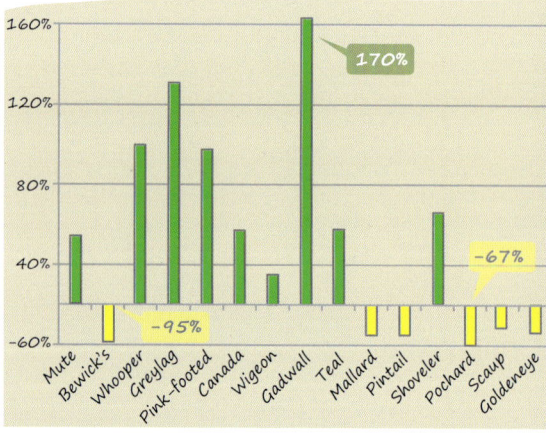

~ WINTERING WATERFOWL ~

Above shows the population trend seen for some of the UK's main waterfowl breeding in the UK between the years 1995 & 2015. To the right, the same idea is illustrated for some of the main wintering waterfowl observed from 1989/90-2014/15. Although the overall picture would appear positive, there are a number of waterfowl species such as the breeding Shelduck and wintering Pochard populations in greater need of our help.

10 FUN FACTS

1. The name for a group of ducks on land is a 'brace', whereas in flight a 'flock' and on water a 'raft', 'team', 'paddling' or even 'badling'.

2. For geese, the terms 'flock' or 'gaggle' are used when on ground & 'skein' in flight.

3. Swans are referred to as a 'bevy' when on land or water and in flight the name 'wedge' is used.

4. The feet of ducks, geese and swans do have nerves and blood vessels in their feet. Cooler blood flows through the feet providing food and oxygen and is just warm enough to avoid frostbite.

5. A special gland called the uropygial or simply 'preen gland' is found near the tail. This secretes an oil which acts as a waterproofing agent and waterfowl rub all over their bodies with their heads.

6. Waterfowl have three types of feathers. The 'contours' act as the birds' protective outer shield, the 'flight feathers' on the tail & wings enable flight as the name suggests. The innermost layer of feathers is for insulation, such as the 'down', historically coming from Eider ducks.

7. Scientific literature suggests Mallards have around 12,000 feathers.

8. Waterfowl are found everywhere in the world except the Antarctic. The South Georgian Pintail duck ventures to the Antarctic coasts but doesn't stay there long enough to be considered a resident.

9. Waterfowl have colour vision.

10. Males have the bright coloured plumage to attract the females which in turn need the brown tone of feathers to remain camouflaged whilst nesting.

Quiz Time

A few questions to further your swan knowledge

1. The Mute swan is the largest waterfowl in the UK; males weigh up to 10kg. But which is the largest in the world?

2. Feathers make up around one-sixth of the weight of a bird. To the nearest thousand, how many feathers on average do swans have?

3. The time that ducks incubate eggs varies between 18 & 35 days, but how many do swans incubate for?

4. For centuries, Mute swans have been known as 'birds royal'. Why do you think this is?

5. Every July a ceremony called 'Swan Upping' takes place. What do you think this event is for?

6. What is the main difference between swans found north of the equator versus those found south of it?

Turn to page 150 to find out the answers.

THE SWANS

Swans belong to the sub-family Anatidae, known as Anserinae. The males and females of all species have identical plumages, with the larger size of males being the only difference. They are described as monogamous, meaning pairs will generally stay together for life. Divorce does sometimes occur due to successional breeding failures. The number of eggs in each clutch ranges from 3-8. Unlike ducks, swans moult once a year, typically in late July or early August.

Both male (cob) and female (pen) are involved in rearing the young. Outside breeding, swans tend to be highly gregarious, forming large colonies. Breeding can be equally colonial, with the exception of the Mute Swan which tends to be more territorial. There are eight species of swan across the world, four occurring in Great Britain, whilst the others are native to North & South America: Trumpeter, Coscoroba, Whistling and Black-necked.

Swans are amongst some of the largest flying birds in the world, all featuring long necks and strong bills for grazing terrestrial and aquatic vegetation.

Wow Fact!
Females moult before males to ensure one parent is always best able to defend the family against predators.

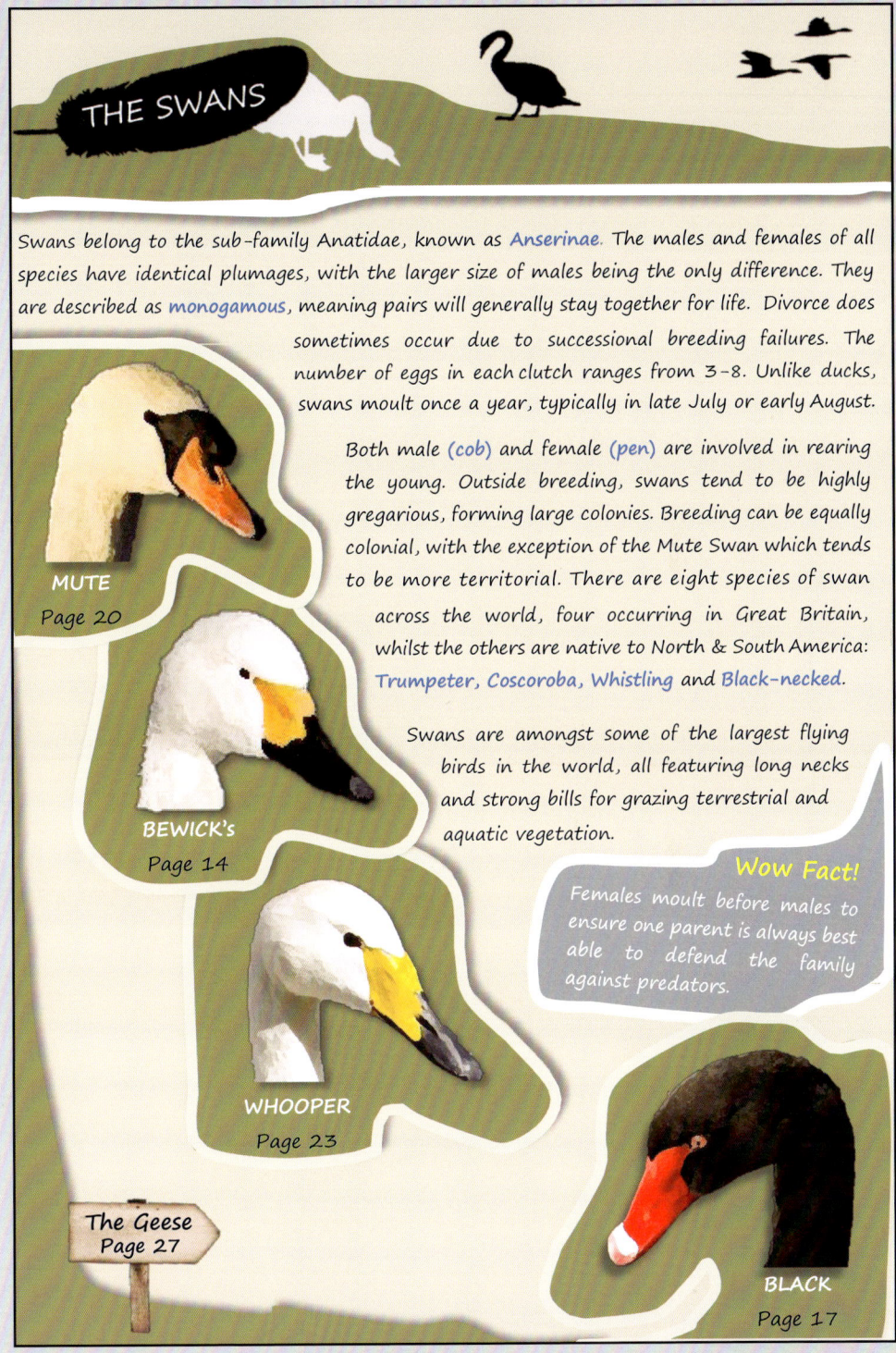

MUTE — Page 20

BEWICK's — Page 14

WHOOPER — Page 23

BLACK — Page 17

The Geese — Page 27

Bewick's swan

Bewick's Swan
Cygnus columbianus

ENDANGERED
EN

Did you know?

The Bewick's swan takes its name from the acclaimed wood engraver, artist and naturalist Thomas Bewick who lived from 1753-1828.

ABOUT

DESCRIPTION

The Bewick's swan is the smallest of the swans in Britain. Males and females differ in size but have identical plumage; youngsters are grey with pinkish bills.

BEHAVIOUR

Often migrate and winter in family parties. This can be up to four generations; joining with other families to form large congregations. They are comfortable on land, Bewick's spend more time grazing than the other swans.

HABITAT

Large estuaries and shallow tundra pools in Siberia are used. In winter, they prefer shallower coastal areas, estuaries and flooded meadows, including the WWT Slimbridge centre.

VOICE

A softer and more musical resonance than Whoopers; when alarmed, a 'howk' is repeated.

BREEDING

Small islands along river estuaries, plus lakes and the edges of tundra pools.

The 'WHEN, WHERE & KEY FACTS'

WHEN TO SEE THEM

Arriving in the UK in mid-October after breeding in Siberia, Bewick's swans spend winter here, departing in March.

BEST LOCATIONS

Most are found in the east of England, but also around the Severn estuary, the Ouse & Nene washes in Cambridgeshire. The WWT centres of Slimbridge and Martin Mere are key sites.

UK DISTRIBUTION

LIFESPAN ~ 10 YEARS ~

SOCIABILITY ~ FLOCKS ~

SUMMER ~ N/A
WINTER ~ 7,000 individuals

POPULATION STATUS

ADULT

CYGNET

Black swan

Black Swan
Cygnus atratus

LEAST CONCERN
LC

Did you know?

The Black swan features on the coat of arms of the state of Western Australia. They also form part of the state's flag within a yellow disc.

ABOUT

DESCRIPTION

On water, it appears entirely black with a curled-cum-ruffled plumage. Only in flight do the white primary wings show. The waxy crimson-red bill is white at its tip.

BEHAVIOUR

Unlike the Bewick's swan, the Black swan does not venture onto land as often. Their take-off into the air can also appear slightly awkward at times. Black swans are quite active at dusk, often with a trumpet-like call.

HABITAT

In their native Australia, they choose large lakes and brackish or fresh water lagoons, estuaries & sheltered coastal bays. In the UK, larger water bodies & flooded ground are preferred.

VOICE

Black swans possess a high-pitched voice. Short conversational notes are heard if in closer proximity.

BREEDING

In Australia, large community nests are common. Males help with the incubation.

The 'WHEN, WHERE & KEY FACTS'

WHEN TO SEE THEM

A small feral population exists in the UK. Breeding success is however limited as birds tend to nest in the autumn season.

BEST LOCATIONS

There are no well-defined UK locations for Black swans due to the small feral population. Your local wildlife organisation, such as the **Wildlife Trusts,** can advise if birds are present nearby.

UK DISTRIBUTION

LIFESPAN ~ 10 YEARS ~

~ FLOCKS ~ SOCIABILITY

SUMMER ~ 50-100 individuals
WINTER ~ 50-100 individuals

POPULATION STATUS

ADULT

CYGNET

THE SWANS | 19

Mute swan

Mute Swan
Cygnus olor

LEAST CONCERN LC

Did you know?

The unmarked mute swans are regarded as belonging to the Queen. A ceremony of 'swan upping' takes place during the 3rd week of July each year.

ABOUT

DESCRIPTION

Mute swans differ from other swans of the northern hemisphere due to their reddish rather than yellow bill, and their curved neck and pointed tail feathers.

BEHAVIOUR

Often likened to a sailing boat because of the arched wings and raised tail feathers.

Mute swans are more sedentary than Bewick's and Whooper swans. During breeding times, they are territorial & hence you are unlikely to see groups of them.

HABITAT

Mute swans are found in almost all habitats: reservoirs, ponds, lakes, rivers and estuaries. However, when breeding, shallow water sites are chosen with plenty of food available to raise their brood.

VOICE

Adults produce hissing and grunting notes, hence their name 'mute'; cygnets give a weak pipping sound.

BREEDING

Shallow water islands or banks. Young stay with the parents until the following spring.

The 'WHEN, WHERE & KEY FACTS'

WHEN TO SEE THEM

The UK's most numerous and only all-year-round resident. During the past 40 years numbers initially declined due to swallowing of lead fishing weights. Since these were banned by law in 1987, numbers have recovered.

BEST LOCATIONS

Found across most of the UK except for the northern parts of Scotland in the highlands, few birds found in mid-Wales and the moorlands in the south-west of England. Expect to see them in both rural and urban places where a pond, shallow lake or slow-moving watercourse exists.

UK DISTRIBUTION

LIFESPAN ~ 10-15 YEARS ~

~ SMALL FLOCKS ~ SOCIABILITY

SUMMER ~ 7,000 + pairs
WINTER ~ 79,000 Individuals

POPULATION STATUS

ADULT

CYGNET

Whooper swan

Whooper Swan
Cygnus cygnus

LEAST CONCERN LC

Did you know?

The 'Super Whooper', as it is sometimes referred to, is the national bird of Finland and also features on the Finnish 1 Euro coin.

ABOUT

DESCRIPTION
The largest swan to occur in the UK; often confused with the Bewick's swan. Along with their greater size, each have unique bill patterns and the yellow extends more.

BEHAVIOUR
Are less domesticated than the Mute swan, more like the Bewick's swan. Their neck is often straight when alerted & more curved when feeding or aggressive. Although at ease on land, more time is spent on water for feeding & resting.

HABITAT
Preference for large estuaries and shallow tundra pools when breeding. Otherwise, shallow coastal areas, estuaries and flooded meadows are preferred. The WWT reserve in Slimbridge attracts many winter visitors.

VOICE
As the name suggests, Whooper swans have a double-noted bugling voice, with a higher pitched second note.

BREEDING
Bulky nests in the Icelandic taiga zone are bound by mud, mosses and grasses.

The 'WHEN, WHERE & KEY FACTS'

WHEN TO SEE THEM
Arrive in October from subarctic Eurasia; further south than the Bewick's in the taiga zone. They head north-west again in March.

BEST LOCATIONS
East Scotland, northern England, the RSPB Ouse washes in Cambridgeshire as well as Norfolk are key locations. The loughs of Neagh & Beg in Northern Ireland are also popular wintering sites.

UK DISTRIBUTION

LIFESPAN ~ 10 YEARS ~

SOCIABILITY ~ FLOCKS ~

SUMMER ~ 9-14 pairs
WINTER ~ 15,000 individuals

POPULATION STATUS

ADULT

CYGNET

THE SWANS | 25

Quiz Time

Have a gander at these goose related questions!

1. What is the name of the highest-flying goose in the world?

2. Based on both height & weight, which is the largest goose resident in Britain?

3. What is the reason for geese flying in a "V" formation?

4. Which species of goose has specially adapted glands, enabling them to drink saltier waters?

5. Which species of goose, not native to Britain, has successfully established a strong breeding population here?

6. For its annual migration, which species of goose covers the greatest distance to visit Britain?

Turn to page 151 to find out the answers.

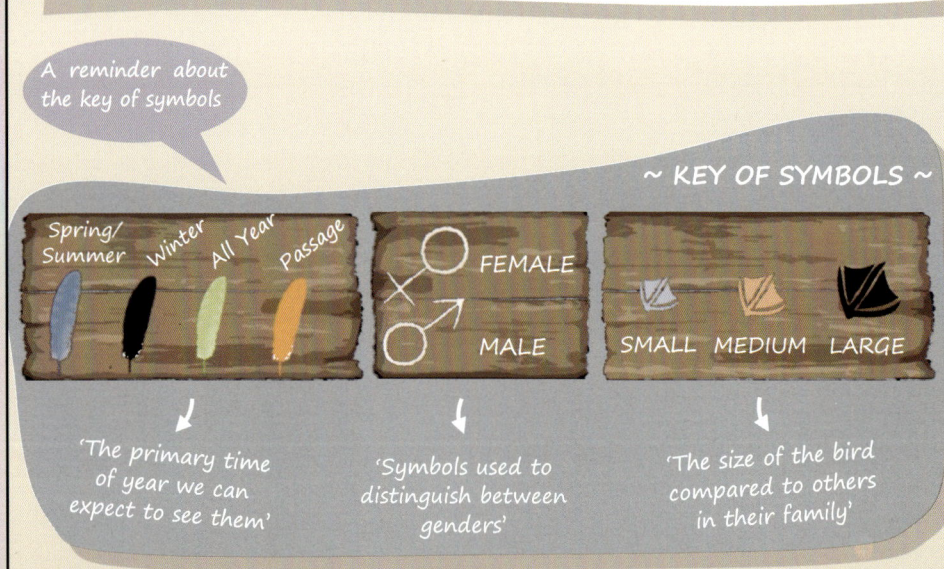

A reminder about the key of symbols

~ KEY OF SYMBOLS ~

Spring/Summer | Winter | All Year | Passage

FEMALE
MALE

SMALL   MEDIUM   LARGE

'The primary time of year we can expect to see them'

'Symbols used to distinguish between genders'

'The size of the bird compared to others in their family'

26 | THE GEESE

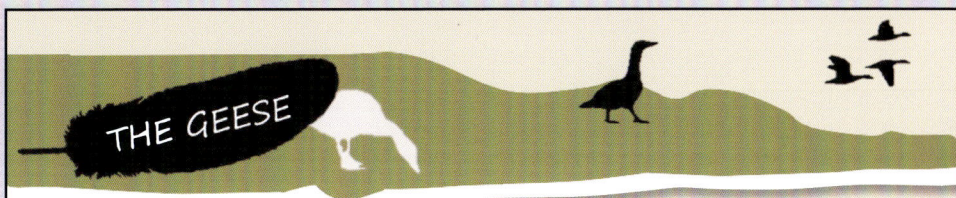

THE GEESE

Like the swans, geese are also part of the Anserinae tribe, the sub-family of the overarching Anatidae family. In terms of size, the majority of geese fit between the other two family members, the swans and ducks, with one or two exceptions. The tribe is split into three further groups, placing each species into its relevant genus (the taxonomic classification).

Geese Genera

BRANTA — Barnacle, Brent, Canada

ANSER — Bean, Greylag, Pink-footed, White-fronted

CHEN — Snow

The word goose is derived from the Proto-Indo-European language, which is the family of languages spoken over the greater part of Europe, Asia and as far as northern India. In old English, **'gôs'**, **'gandres'** and **'ges'** became goose, gander and geese in modern English. Geese are primarily terrestrial birds with most of their feeding taking place on grassland, but the raiding of farmland crops during the winter is also common. Their strong bills with 'toothed' edges (lamellae) on the upper mandible are perfectly adapted for cutting & grazing.

Wow Fact!

Geese are very caring. Should one become sick or wounded on migration, others will withdraw from the group to look after their mate until they recover.

The Ducks Page 53

The Egyptian goose is now well established in the UK. They are members of the Sheldgeese & Shelduck tribe known as Tadorninae.

Egyptian — ALOPOCHEN

Barnacle goose

Barnacle Goose
Branta leucopsis

LEAST CONCERN
LC

ABOUT

Did you know?

Once an important part of medieval cuisine because it was believed that they had been produced from the Barnacle, therefore Catholics could eat their flesh with impunity during lent.

DESCRIPTION

The Barnacle goose has a creamy-white face and forehead with a black streak between the beak & eye. The rest of body is darker, such as the crown and neck; the underparts are grey, and faint barred flanks. In flight, a v-shaped white rump patch and silver-grey under wing linings can be seen. Sexes are alike.

BEHAVIOUR

Very sociable birds, often gathering in flocks of thousands in winter. Solitary birds may be seen with grey geese groups instead.

HABITAT

Rocky coastal regions, small islands and marshes are common. In winter, coastal pastures, tidal flats & even cultivated farm-land at times too.

VOICE

Males have short high-pitched barks, whilst females have a much deeper voice of similar frequency.

BREEDING

Begins in May-June. Breeding pairs are quite colonial; many nests found close to one another. These are usually placed on the face of steep cliffs, rocky outcrops or low-lying islands.

The 'WHEN, WHERE & KEY FACTS'

WHEN TO SEE THEM
From mid-October to March. Two distinct populations arrive from breeding grounds in Greenland and Svalbard, Norway.

BEST LOCATIONS
Those arriving from Greenland overwinter on the Hebrides of western Scotland and western Ireland, whilst the other population from Svalbard overwinters in the Solway Firth.

UK DISTRIBUTION

LIFESPAN ~ 18 YEARS ~

SOCIABILITY ~ SMALL FLOCKS ~

SUMMER ~ 900 pairs
WINTER ~ 94,000 individuals

POPULATION STATUS

ADULT

GOSLING

58,000 ~ Greenland
33,000 ~ Svalbard
3,000 ~ UK Feral birds

Bean Goose

Bean Goose
Anser fabalis

LEAST CONCERN LC

ABOUT

Did you know?

The collective term used to describe the Bean goose is a 'pod'. Their name comes from the reputation for grazing in bean field stubbles during the winter.

DESCRIPTION

The plumage of the Bean goose is more uniform than that of the other grey geese; it is lacking the paler forewing of the Greylag goose and the dark markings of the White-fronted goose. Due to the variety of bill colours and shapes, there are five sub-species recognised, three in the Taiga and two in the Tundra.

BEHAVIOUR

Except for the Greylags, this is the largest of the grey geese, but also the most silent. They tend to roost inland, usually on lakes and marshes.

HABITAT

Present in Britain during the winter, Bean geese inhabit estuaries, seashores, stubble and pastures.

VOICE

Two-noted call, not dissimilar to the Greylag's; more like the call of the Pink-footed goose. It is though a deeper and more of a 'honking' tune.

BREEDING

Breeding occurs in northern Scandinavia, Russia and Asia. Only very rarely as visitors to Britain during the autumn & winter.

The 'WHEN, WHERE & KEY FACTS'

WHEN TO SEE THEM

Most of the UK's Bean geese arrive from the Scandinavian region in late September and depart again in March.

BEST LOCATIONS

The Yare Valley in Norfolk is the principal location, including the RSPB's Mid-Yare nature reserves. Southern Scotland near Falkirk hosts another population of Bean geese.

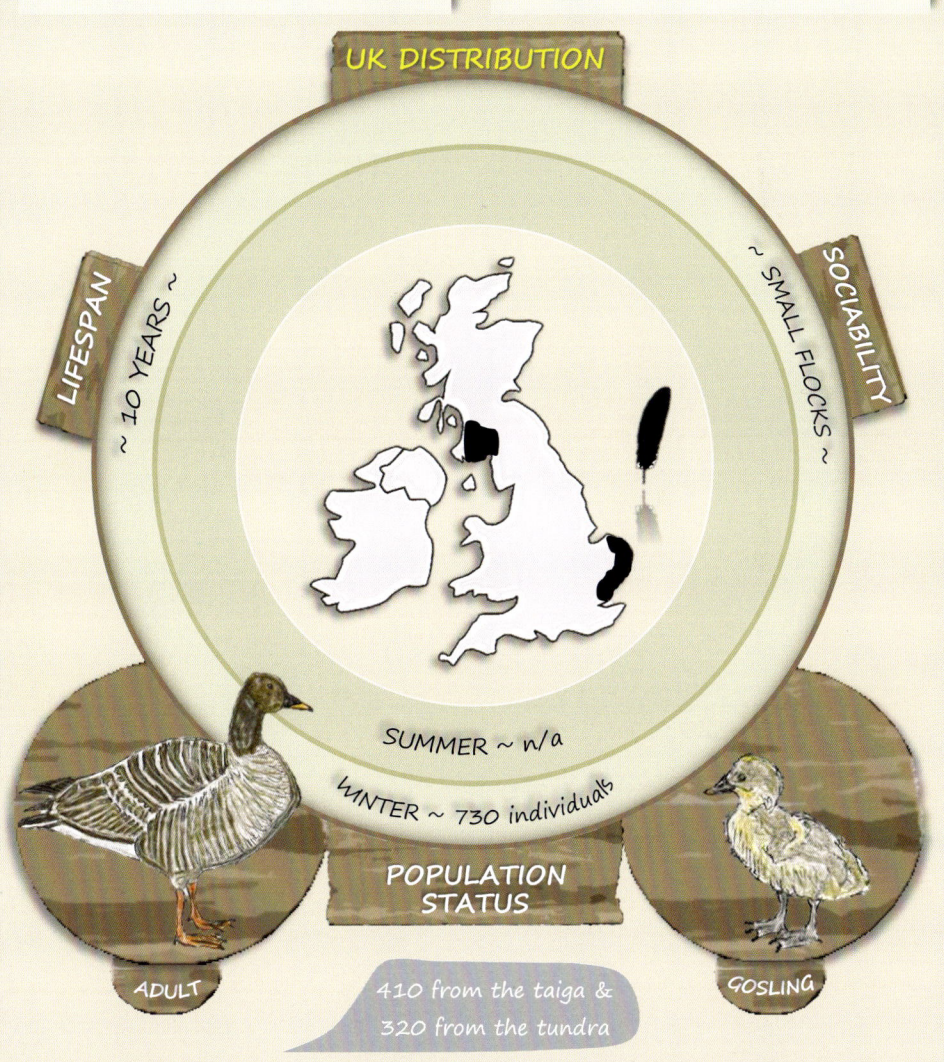

UK DISTRIBUTION

LIFESPAN ~ 10 YEARS ~

SOCIABILITY ~ SMALL FLOCKS ~

SUMMER ~ n/a
WINTER ~ 730 individuals

POPULATION STATUS

410 from the taiga & 320 from the tundra

ADULT

GOSLING

Brent Goose

Brent Goose
Branta bernicla

LEAST CONCERN LC

ABOUT

Did you know?
Unlike most other geese, Brent geese possess highly developed salt glands that allow them to drink salt water. They also have the shortest tail of any goose.

DESCRIPTION
The plumage of the Brent goose is predominantly black and white. The neck features a patchy white collar, with tail coverts & the sides of the rump also white. Their flanks have a pale grey barring.

BEHAVIOUR
Highly maritime, in other words, spending most of their time on coastal sea waters. The movement of the tides determine their feeding time – day or night – depending on when the tide is out.

HABITAT
The offshore islands, marshy uplands and tundra lakes are favoured for breeding, whereas in winter habitats include muddy estuaries, tidal bays and marshy uplands.

VOICE
A husky honking is given out, which is commonly described as a 'kkronk' noise.

BREEDING
Unfortunately, Brents do not breed in the UK. Two sub-species arrive here in the winter. The light-bellied race breeds in Arctic North America & the dark-bellied race in north-west Siberia.

The 'WHEN, WHERE & KEY FACTS'

WHEN TO SEE THEM
From mid-October to March. The two populations arrive from its breeding locations in Greenland, Canada and Svalbard.

BEST LOCATIONS
Dark-bellied mainly on the Wash in north Norfolk plus the Essex & Thames estuaries. Most Light-bellied birds reside on the Strangford Lough & Lough Foyle in N. Ireland and Lindisfarne, Northumberland.

UK DISTRIBUTION

LIFESPAN ~ 10 YEARS ~

SOCIABILITY ~ SMALL FLOCKS ~

SUMMER ~ n/a
WINTER ~ 121,400 individuals

POPULATION STATUS

91,000 ~ Dark-bellied
30,400 ~ Light-bellied

ADULT

GOSLING

Canada Goose
Branta canadensis

LEAST CONCERN LC

ABOUT

Did you know?
Thirteen distinct calls are said to have been identified for the Canada goose. The epithet 'canadensis' from their Latin name is actually a new Latin word which means 'from Canada'.

DESCRIPTION
The Canada goose is the largest wild goose in the UK. It has a distinctive black neck and head, along with white cheeks & throat patch. It was first introduced to the UK from North America in the late 17th century for King James II's collection of waterfowl in St. James Park, London.

BEHAVIOUR
Canada geese spend an equal amount of time on land grazing & in water where they reach down for silt.

HABITAT
During the summer, marshes, wet & dry tundra, prairies (large open grassland) and coastal areas. In the winter, open country, fields, edges of ponds or lakes, and estuaries.

VOICE
Like no other species of goose, adults have a reverberating honk; youngsters a cackle.

BREEDING
Canadas may breed as early as March if weather allows. The goslings will leave the nest on the 1st or 2nd day after hatching, being led to water by both parents.

The 'WHEN, WHERE & KEY FACTS'

WHEN TO SEE THEM
Resident all year round with additional birds arriving in the winter. Vagrant Canada goose sub-species may also be seen with other wild geese over the winter.

BEST LOCATIONS
Found in a wide variety of habitats across the whole of the UK, except for the mountainous highland regions of northern Scotland. In winter, the smaller vagrant Canada races may be seen with other wild geese; most often in N. Ireland & W. Scotland.

UK DISTRIBUTION

~ LIFESPAN ~ 20-25 YEARS ~

~ SOCIABILITY ~ SMALL FLOCKS ~

SUMMER ~ 62,000 pairs
WINTER ~ 190,000 individuals

POPULATION STATUS

ADULT

GOSLING

Egyptian Goose

Egyptian Goose
Alopochen aegyptiacus

LEAST CONCERN LC

Did you know?
Originally the result of a cross breeding between a goose and a duck. They were domesticated by the ancient Egyptians as they considered them to be sacred.

ABOUT

DESCRIPTION
First brought to the UK in the 18th century, where after some escaped from captivity to establish a feral population. Related to the Shelduck, Egyptian geese have an unmistakable brown eye patch, grey-pale brown plumage and contrasting stark white upper wing coverts.

BEHAVIOUR
Quite vocal birds that are normally found in pairs or small groups. During breeding they are more territorial & aggressive.

HABITAT
Marshy areas, small ponds, lakes as well as the banks of rivers are preferred sites since establishing in the wild in the UK.

VOICE
Males have a hoarse breathing voice like someone with a sore throat; females sound a harsh trumpeting.

BREEDING
Cavities of trees and abandoned nests of other birds are often selected; ledges on cliffs & river banks too. Goslings are similarly marked to that of the Shelduck gosling.

THE GEESE | 41

The 'WHEN, WHERE & KEY FACTS'

WHEN TO SEE THEM
Feral populations of the Egyptian goose in the UK are resident here all year round and are non-migratory.

BEST LOCATIONS
Originally brought to the UK as an ornamental bird for captive collections. Since escaping, feral numbers have established well at Holkham Park in north Norfolk & Regents Park in central London.

UK DISTRIBUTION

~ LIFESPAN ~ 15 YEARS ~

~ SOCIABILITY ~ SMALL FLOCKS ~

SUMMER ~ 1,100 pairs
WINTER ~ 3,400 individuals

POPULATION STATUS

ADULT

GOSLING

Greylag Goose

Greylag Goose
Anser anser

LEAST CONCERN LC

ABOUT

Did you know?
The 'lag' portion of the name developed from the fact that they are always one of the last geese to begin their migration. In other words, 'lagging behind'.

DESCRIPTION
Ancestor to domestic geese in Europe and North America. They are bulkier than the Canada goose; overall size & weight is less. During the 19th century numbers of Greylags had sharply declined due to over-hunting.

BEHAVIOUR
Very gregarious and often seen in family groups or flocks of many thousands. Their flight is strong and in formation when flying for long distances.

HABITAT
For breeding, low-land marshes, open moor-land, reed marsh & offshore islands are chosen. At other times, salt & fresh water marsh, estuaries, and pasture or stubble field.

VOICE
The most well-known three-noted 'honk', typical of the farm yard goose. A lower pitch note is heard during conversation.

BREEDING
Starts around mid-April. The nest site is often a depression in the ground amongst heather, reeds and rushes. Young fledge in around 8 weeks.

44 | THE GEESE

The 'WHEN, WHERE & KEY FACTS'

WHEN TO SEE THEM

Resident in the UK all year round in the south. In the north, wild visitors mainly occur between September and March or April.

BEST LOCATIONS

Resident in most lowland areas, most commonly grassy fields along river valleys. Wild greylags occur mostly north of the Solway Firth and can be seen at RSPB sites such as Mersehead & Insh Marshes.

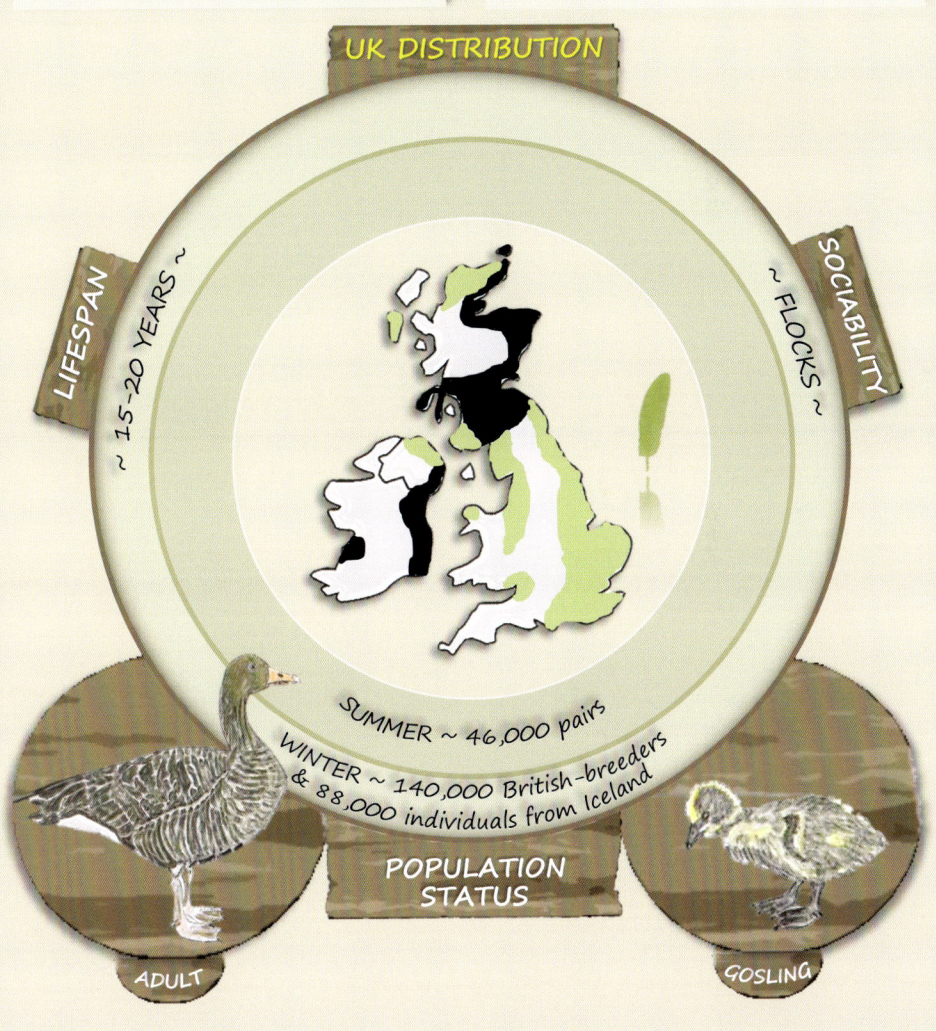

UK DISTRIBUTION

~ LIFESPAN ~ 15-20 YEARS ~

~ SOCIABILITY ~ FLOCKS ~

SUMMER ~ 46,000 pairs
WINTER ~ 140,000 British-breeders & 88,000 individuals from Iceland

POPULATION STATUS

ADULT

GOSLING

THE GEESE | 45

Pink-Footed Goose

Pink-footed Goose
Anser brachyrhynchus

LEAST CONCERN LC

ABOUT

Did you know?

In 1951, Sir Peter Scott and his team undertook an expedition to Iceland to seek the breeding grounds of the Pink-footed goose. They also discovered that all the geese wintered in the UK.

DESCRIPTION

Considered to be a sub-species of the Bean goose, but somewhat smaller. Besides unique pink bills & feet, they also have paler grey backs. The head & neck are very dark, boldly contrasting with their pale forewings in flight.

BEHAVIOUR

Highly sociable birds throughout winter and during breeding. The winter roosts are often on large sand banks or estuaries, also lakes & marshes when there is little disturbance.

HABITAT

During breeding, river valleys, swampy plains, & rocky coastal areas are chosen on the islands of Spitsbergen, Iceland & Greenland. In winter, often found close to estuaries & cultivated farmland & moorlands.

VOICE

A variably pitched two- or three-noted call; not as high as White-fronts. A very high-pitched squeal is sounded when alarmed.

BREEDING

Nests are usually a shallow depression on the ground filled with grass, moss & a down lining. Nests may be used for consecutive years.

THE GEESE | 47

The 'WHEN, WHERE & KEY FACTS'

WHEN TO SEE THEM

The main population from Iceland & Greenland overwinter almost exclusively in the UK. They spend from October to April here.

BEST LOCATIONS

Large estuaries are favoured, including those on the east Scottish coast. Other sites include the Wash in North Norfolk, Solway and Ribble estuaries. Also farmland during the day for feeding.

UK DISTRIBUTION

LIFESPAN ~ 10 YEARS ~

SOCIABILITY ~ SMALL FLOCKS ~

SUMMER ~ n/a

WINTER ~ 360,000 individuals

POPULATION STATUS

ADULT

GOSLING

48 | THE GEESE

White-fronted goose

White-fronted Goose
Anser albifrons

LEAST CONCERN LC

Did you know?

Also known as the Greater White-fronted goose in North America, this species has one of the largest ranges of all the world's geese. There are five subspecies recognised, two of which visit the UK.

ABOUT

DESCRIPTION

A darker and slightly smaller goose than the Greylag. The main feature is the white patch at the base of the bill. The front of the neck and underparts are greyer with black irregular barring on breast & belly. Feathers also show a paler edging. The Greenland race has a more orange-yellow bill and feet compared to the pink of European birds.

BEHAVIOUR

More agile & acrobatic in flight than other grey geese. They can spring almost vertically into the air upon take-off from the ground.

HABITAT

Whilst overwintering in the UK, open country is preferred. This includes agricultural land like stubble fields, but also wet meadows, fresh water and even brackish marshy habitats.

VOICE

Compared to other grey geese, White-fronts have a higher pitched, more musical and faster delivered 2 or 3-noted call. Also called the speckle-belly or laughing goose.

BREEDING

The European birds breed mainly in Siberia and the other in Greenland as the name would suggest.

The 'WHEN, WHERE & KEY FACTS'

WHEN TO SEE THEM

Both races arrive in the UK in October from their respective Siberian and Greenland breeding sites. They stay here until March.

BEST LOCATIONS

For the European race, southern England, particularly the Severn estuary in Gloucester and the Swale estuary, Kent, are good. Greenland birds are found in west Scotland and Ireland; especially Wexford in the south-east.

UK DISTRIBUTION

LIFESPAN ~ 15–20 YEARS ~

~ SMALL FLOCKS ~ SOCIABILITY

SUMMER ~ n/a
WINTER ~ 2,400: European race
13,000 individuals: Greenland race

POPULATION STATUS

ADULT

GOSLING

Quiz Time

Can you answer these questions like a duck takes to water?

1. Which duck, occurring in the UK, has the greatest flying speed?

2. Most duck feathers change to an 'eclipse plumage'. What is the purpose of this?

3. Are ducks purely herbivores, i.e. eating only the plant matter available in and around ponds & lakes?

4. Many ducks in the UK dive underwater for food. Which species dives to the greatest depth?

5. After the Mallard, which is the most common duck to over-winter in the UK?

6. Is it true that ducks are found on every continent in the world?

Turn to page 152 to find out the answers.

What were all those symbols again?

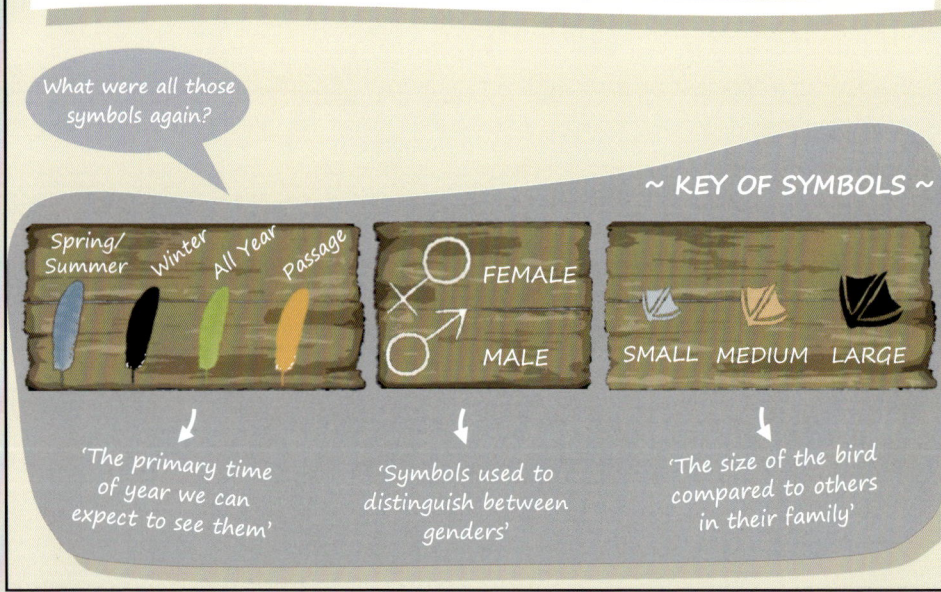

~ KEY OF SYMBOLS ~

Spring/Summer | Winter | All Year | Passage

FEMALE
MALE

SMALL MEDIUM LARGE

'The primary time of year we can expect to see them'

'Symbols used to distinguish between genders'

'The size of the bird compared to others in their family'

52 | THE DUCKS

THE DUCKS

Unlike swans and geese, the ducks make up their own sub-family called the Anatinae, under the overarching Anatidae family. Not only is this the largest of the two sub-families within the waterfowl grouping but also shows the greatest variation between species. Despite the distinct characteristics of each tribe of ducks, they all possess a number of common physical attributes. Ducks from five of the ten worldwide tribes occur in the UK, either as residents or seasonal migrants.

Duck Tribes

DABBLING DUCKS — Mallard, Shoveler, Gadwall, Garganey, Pintail, Teal, Wigeon

DIVING DUCKS — Tufted, Scaup, Pochard

SHELDUCKS — Shelduck

SEA DUCKS — Smew, Eider, Goldeneye, Goosander, Merganser, Long-tailed

PERCHING DUCKS — Mandarin, Carolina

There is a clear sexual dimorphism between the plumages of ducks; in other words, the male (drake) and female (duck) possess very different coloured feathers. The males are much more brightly patterned due to their role in attracting their partners during the courtship display. The females have evolved much drabber plumage as a result of their role sitting on the nest incubating the brood, thereby providing enhanced better camouflaging from potential predators.

A further sexual dimorphism relates to the voices of ducks. Males have asymmetrically enlarged Windpipes, hence the higher-pitched call produced by them compared to the deeper note of the ducks. Before any mating takes place, pairs of ducks carry out a courtship display, not seen between geese or swans. Yet, the bonds between pairs rarely carries over to successive breeding seasons; swans, however, are known for their monogamy (long-term relationships). Every species of duck has a unique behaviour that enables us to identify them and to assign them to the different tribes.

Carolina Wood Duck

♂

♀

Carolina Wood Duck
Aix sponsa

LEAST CONCERN LC

Did you know?
Artificial nest boxes were first put up in the 1930s to help boost the rebounding Wood duck population which had suffered from habitat loss and hunting for the ladies' hats market in Europe.

ABOUT

DESCRIPTION
Males have long, dark and drooping crests, which in good light show glossy green. There are white marks on the face & between the speckled chestnut breast and pale orange flanks. Virtually every feather has an ornate marking. Females are similar to the Mandarin; mostly grey to dark-brown colour, but with a larger white eye ring.

BEHAVIOUR
Quite tame and unwary birds, which prefer spending time on land and perching on trees. When they swim, the head jerks back and forth like a pigeon.

HABITAT
Carolinas prefer the shallow waters with plenty of surrounding woodland & cover like the related Mandarin.

VOICE
The male produces an intermittent soft and squeaky 'jeeb', whilst the female, particularly when nest searching, produces a fast-paced 'tetetetet'.

BREEDING
As perching ducks, they nest in tree cavities; often competing with other UK birds. They breed in eastern North America, also Cuba and South British Columbia.

THE DUCKS | 55

The 'WHEN, WHERE & KEY FACTS'

WHEN TO SEE THEM

Small numbers of feral ducks have existed in the UK since the late 19th century following escapes from captive collections. They have yet to establish a significant population to be considered on the British list.

BEST LOCATIONS

Carolina Wood ducks regularly escape from captive collections like their related species the Mandarin. Self-sustaining populations have not established to the same extent as the Mandarin and so there are as yet no well-defined locations in the UK.

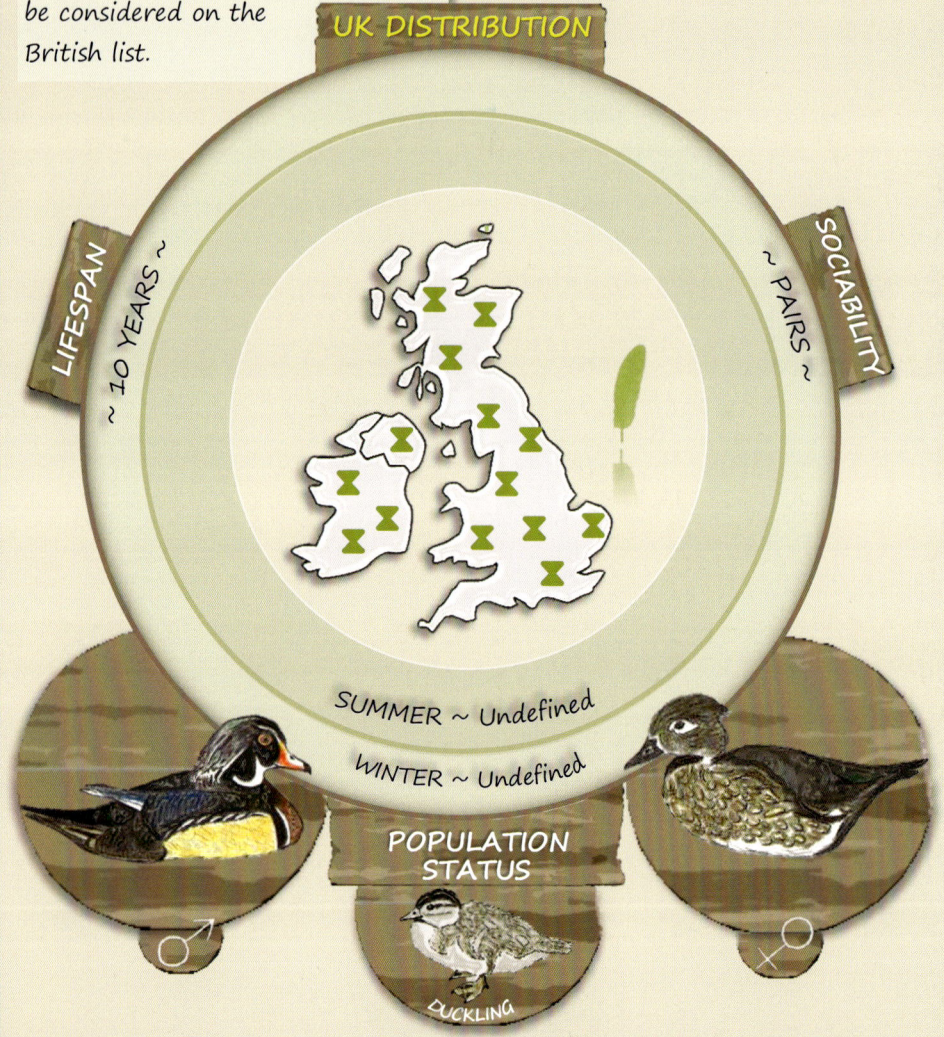

UK DISTRIBUTION

LIFESPAN ~ 10 YEARS ~

SOCIABILITY ~ PAIRS ~

SUMMER ~ Undefined
WINTER ~ Undefined

POPULATION STATUS

DUCKLING

56 | THE DUCKS

Common Scoter

Common Scoter
Melanitta nigra

LEAST CONCERN LC

ABOUT

Did you know?

Divided into two subspecies. In Europe, it is referred to as the 'Common Scoter' and in the USA as the 'Black Scoter'. They are among the most vocal of waterfowl, but also the UK's most threatened of species.

DESCRIPTION

Drakes are completely glossy black. The beak features a black knob at the top & towards the tip there is an area of yellow-orange. Their American counterpart show more of this coloured patch which extends beyond the nostrils. Females are a dusky brown and have this paleness from below the eye to mid-neck. The beak is black with no other features.

BEHAVIOUR

Rarely seen on land, except for breeding. They dive frequently underwater for prey, including molluscs and aquatic insects; a little vegetation is also eaten.

HABITAT

Higher ground is preferred for breeding, but near water. Winter is spent mainly upon coastal waters, however lakes & estuaries too.

VOICE

Much more vocal than the other scoters. The males have a musical call & a more plaintive one too. Ducks make the typical growling noise of diving ducks.

BREEDING

Not common breeders in the UK. Breed in Iceland, Greenland, Scandinavia & much of Russia. The edges of ponds, lakes and even islands are the usual nesting sites.

The 'WHEN, WHERE & KEY FACTS'

WHEN TO SEE THEM

Resident on UK-coastal waters all year. Most birds winter here from October until March. June & July are the two months for breeding.

BEST LOCATIONS

Numbers having dropped by more than half over the last 25 years or so. The West Highland glens of Scotland see a few breeding pairs, the rest are in the blanket bogs in the Flow Country of far northern Scotland. Most of the UK coast hosts Common Scoter colonies in winter. The bays of Carmarthen and Cardigan, Moray Firth and N. Norfolk see the largest gatherings.

UK DISTRIBUTION

~ LIFESPAN ~ 10-15 YEARS ~

~ SOCIABILITY ~ LARGE FLOCKS ~

SUMMER ~ 52 pairs
WINTER ~ 100,000 individuals

POPULATION STATUS

DUCKLING

THE DUCKS | 59

EIDER

Eider
Somateria mollissima

LEAST CONCERN LC

Did you know?
The largest duck by weight in the northern hemisphere. People in Iceland, Siberia and Scandinavia provide nest sites & protection to Eider to collect their 'down' feathers for expensive insulation products such as duvets.

ABOUT

DESCRIPTION
Breeding males have black crowns extending just below the eye with a lime-green patch on nape & side of head. Upperparts, cheeks & throat are white, but from closer view have a pinkish taint. Besides their underparts, the tail & flight feathers are visible as black. The female has a light & dark brown, boldly barred plumage; less so on head and breast.

BEHAVIOUR
Strong fliers and tend to stay low to the water. Rocks & sandbars often used to rest. When on land they walk with a slow-paced and proud posture.

HABITAT
Outside breeding, Eider are almost entirely maritime. Sheltered coastal terrain, coves, bays & islets of estuaries are inhabited otherwise.

VOICE
An unmistakable call described as 'a-oooo'; a muffled cooing that is sounded by the males during certain displays.

BREEDING
Eider are one of the most colonial nesters; a particular reason for the development of farms in places like Iceland that have used their 'down' feathers for over 1,000 years.

The 'WHEN, WHERE & KEY FACTS'

WHEN TO SEE THEM

In their breeding range, Eider ducks can be seen all year. Whilst the coastal areas south of the breeding areas host Eider throughout the winter with birds arriving in autumn.

BEST LOCATIONS

Breed up the Northumberland coast; especially the Farne Islands as well as Scotland's west coast. The wintering range includes the above, also extending further south down the Yorkshire coast as well as most of the east & south coasts. Belfast Lough, N. Ireland, hosts many birds.

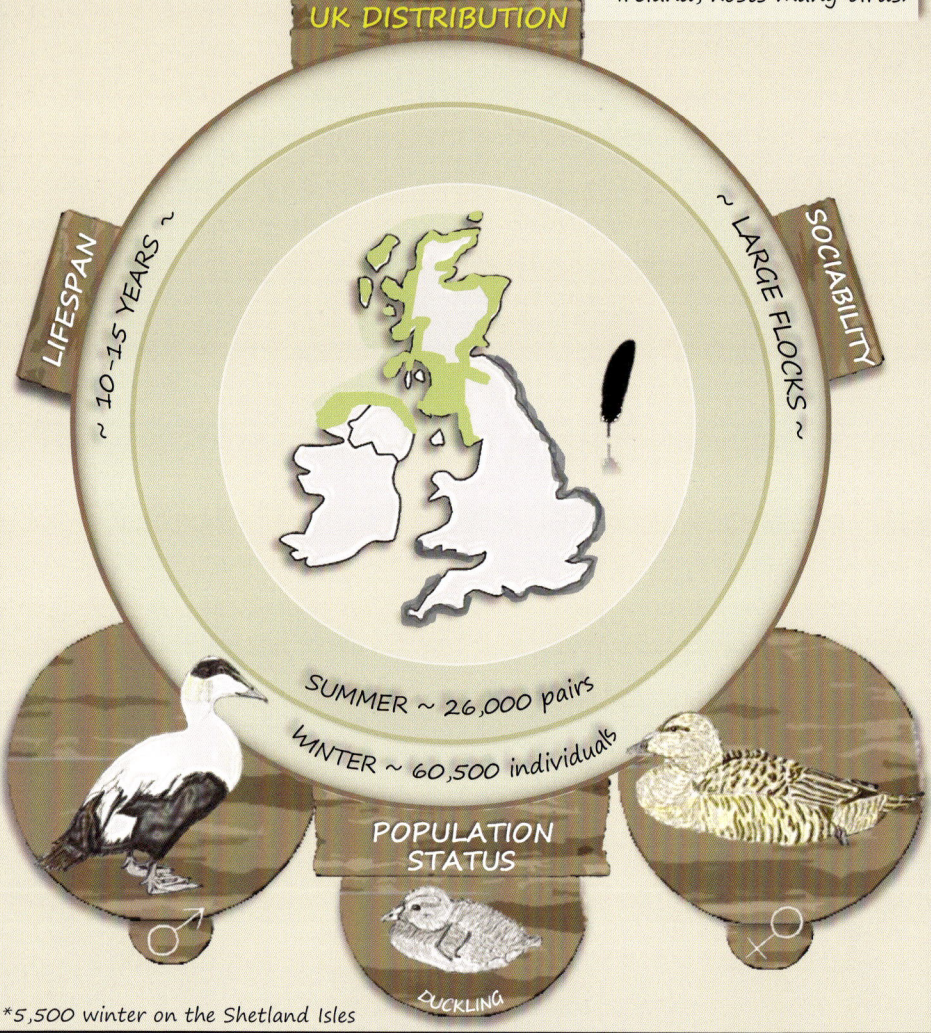

UK DISTRIBUTION

~ LIFESPAN ~ 10-15 YEARS ~

~ SOCIABILITY ~ LARGE FLOCKS ~

SUMMER ~ 26,000 pairs
WINTER ~ 60,500 individuals

POPULATION STATUS

DUCKLING

*5,500 winter on the Shetland Isles

Gadwall

THE DUCKS | 63

Gadwall
Anas strepera

LEAST CONCERN LC

Did you know?
Gadwall are one of the least gregarious and colonial dabbling ducks in the UK. Outside of the breeding season they tend to form only small flocks.

ABOUT

DESCRIPTION
Gadwall are a little smaller than Mallards. The males are grey-brown with a black patch under the tail. Their head & neck is pale buff with brown spots and streaks. Females are patterned brown and buff; both sexes have a pale grey underside. Ducks and drakes have a dark slate grey beak, but the females feature an orange band too.

BEHAVIOUR
Often found in flocks with Mallards. They feed in the typical dabbling duck fashion of up-ending. They swim with tail elevated.

HABITAT
Ponds, lakes, muddy estuary edges, parks, reservoirs and coastal wetlands in winter. Shallow edges of lakes or ponds with much vegetation for breeding.

VOICE
Males have a harsh croaking voice and short & deep sounding calls, females have a quack like Mallards.

BREEDING
Scarcer UK breeders; more in N. Europe, as well as Asia & central North America, from where they arrive in winter. Nests are close to water & concealed in thick vegetation.

The 'WHEN, WHERE & KEY FACTS'

WHEN TO SEE THEM

Present here all year round, but with numbers increasing in the autumn and winter when more birds arrive from the Continent.

BEST LOCATIONS

The best places include the Midlands and south-east England, such as Blashford Lakes, Hampshire, and Amwell, Hertfordshire. Also eastern-central Scotland, eastern N. Ireland and south-east Ireland in Wexford, and south-east Wales.

UK DISTRIBUTION

~ LIFESPAN ~ 10-15 YEARS ~

~ SOCIABILITY ~ FLOCKS ~

SUMMER ~ Up to 1,730 pairs
WINTER ~ 25,000 individuals

POPULATION STATUS

DUCKLING

THE DUCKS | 65

Garganey

Garganey
Anas querquedula

LEAST CONCERN LC

Did you know?

The only species of waterfowl that are entirely summer visitors to the UK. The Swedish botanist and zoologist Linnaeus was the first to describe the Garganey.

ABOUT

DESCRIPTION

Smaller than a Mallard & Gadwall, but bigger than a Teal. Garganey males have dark brown crowns with a rusty brown neck and bold white stripe above the eye, also known as a 'superciliary'. Most of their upperparts are dark brown with pale clean-cut feather edges. Ducks are like the Teal females; mottled & streaked brown & buff, but with white throat.

BEHAVIOUR

Garganey feed mainly by skimming on the water's surface rather than up-ending. Have the agility to spring up off the water like Teal.

HABITAT

Breeds in shallow pools, meres and ditches that are well covered with vegetation. In the winter, they may be seen on the sea, but mostly shallow waters & marsh.

VOICE

Mainly vocal only during the breeding season. Drakes sound a harsh rattling note, females a deep quack.

BREEDING

Garganey are rare UK visitors; small numbers breed in Norfolk & Suffolk. Native to Eurasia, breeding locally in places north of the Pyrenees, the Alps and western Asia.

The 'WHEN, WHERE & KEY FACTS'

WHEN TO SEE THEM

Small numbers of breeding birds visit between March & July. The entire population migrates to India (esp. Santragachi lake, W. Bengal), also S. Africa or Australasia in the winter.

BEST LOCATIONS

Garganey are rare breeders in the UK. Most of them breed on the quiet marshes in Norfolk and Suffolk. In Ireland, a few pairs now breed in Wexford on the south-east coast, some on coast between England & Scotland, and western Wales, too.

UK DISTRIBUTION

~ LIFESPAN ~
~ 10 YEARS ~

~ SOCIABILITY ~
~ FAMILY GROUPS ~

SUMMER ~ Up to 3,800 pairs
WINTER ~ 12,000 individuals

POPULATION STATUS

DUCKLING

68 | THE DUCKS

Goldeneye

Goldeneye
Bucephala clangula

LEAST CONCERN
LC

Did you know?

Females are known to return to the area where they were born, termed 'philopatry'. Once they breed, they often use the same nesting site for consecutive years thereafter.

ABOUT

DESCRIPTION

One of the smaller sea ducks. Breeding males feature white-striped black upperparts. Their head is iridescent glossy green & black with a white cheek spot between the 'goldeneye' and dark grey bill. Females are a little smaller with a grey and black-brown mottling. Their head is chocolate brown with an area of white underneath too. Beak has orange band.

BEHAVIOUR

Frequent divers; often choosing to travel underwater. Goldeneye are swift fliers; their wings produce a unique whistling noise in flight.

HABITAT

For breeding, shallow & slow-running rivers, with vegetation & woodland if possible. Lakes and ponds, too. Sheltered coastal bays & estuaries are used at other times.

VOICE

Mostly muted. Drakes occasionally sound a sharp 'zee-zee' and 'jeee-ep'; ducks the usual diving duck croak.

BREEDING

Tree cavities are the usual choice with nest boxes accepted too. In treeless areas, cavities between rocks & rabbit burrows are used. The young jump from the nest soon after hatch.

The 'WHEN, WHERE & KEY FACTS'

WHEN TO SEE THEM
Mainly in the Scottish Highlands in summer. Many birds arrive from Northern Europe for the winter and return north come February-March in preparation for breeding.

BEST LOCATIONS
During breeding, they are found almost exclusively in the Highlands of Scotland where they first nested in 1970. In the winter, their range covers almost all of the UK, but particularly north & west Britain.

UK DISTRIBUTION

LIFESPAN ~ 8 YEARS ~

SOCIABILITY ~ SMALL FLOCKS ~

SUMMER ~ 200 pairs
WINTER ~ 20,000 individuals

POPULATION STATUS

DUCKLING

Goosander

Goosander
Mergus m. merganser

LEAST CONCERN
LC

ABOUT

Did you know?

Of the three merganser species in the UK, the Goosander is the largest. Also sometimes referred to as 'Sawbills', 'Fish ducks' or just 'Common merganser'.

DESCRIPTION

Males in breeding have a black-green glossy head & upper neck with an even greener crown. Unlike Red-breasted mergansers, they have no crest. In contrast, females have a rich chestnut brown head, crown and neck with a drooping crest. Rest of upper body is bluish-grey & mottled faintly brown. Both have a red sharply hooked beak.

BEHAVIOUR

Quite sociable outside breeding, often seen in groups up to twenty. Easily alarmed and will always make for water when on land.

HABITAT

Overwintering on large unfrozen inland waters as well as fast-flowing rivers, coastal bays & estuaries. Preference overall for fresh water.

VOICE

Both sexes utter a low quack-like call. Males during breeding have a variety of notes; one is a purring call.

BREEDING

Natural sites include the cavities of trees. The introduction of nest boxes has also encouraged breeding. In Iceland, ground nesting occurs in the treeless regions.

The 'WHEN, WHERE & KEY FACTS'

WHEN TO SEE THEM

All year round; more birds are present in winter. Winter birds are mostly found in England, south of the Humber estuary.

BEST LOCATIONS

Breed particularly along rivers in the north and west of Britain. In winter, birds are more restricted to England on unfrozen freshwater lakes, gravel pits and reservoirs. Their love for salmon and trout however has made them an enemy of fishermen.

UK DISTRIBUTION

~ LIFESPAN ~ 8 YEARS ~

~ SOCIABILITY ~ SMALL FLOCKS ~

POPULATION STATUS

SUMMER ~ Up to 3,800 pairs
WINTER ~ 12,000 individuals

DUCKLING

74 | THE DUCKS

Long-tailed Duck

Long-tailed Duck
Clangula hyemalis

VULNERABLE
VU

ABOUT

Did you know?
Formerly known as Oldsquaw; this name is no longer used due to its negative connotations. The name literally means 'old woman' and links to the duck's talkative nature.

DESCRIPTION
Besides their lengthy tails, drakes display 3 different plumages; most handsome in winter when courtship takes place. Mainly black and white with a sooty brown patch on the back of neck. The beak is slate-blue with a pink band. Females are like males in eclipse, paler on head & neck. Their breast & sides are also mottled and barred brown-white.

BEHAVIOUR
The most skilful divers of all sea ducks. Can submerge for up to a minute & 20mtrs deep. Very aquatic & feeding on water close to shore.

HABITAT
Breeds on the Arctic coasts of N. America, Russia, and Iceland & Norway in both tundra & semi-tundra habitats. Absent of areas without lakes and rivers offered.

VOICE
Very vocal, especially through courtship & breeding. Musical notes by both sexes. Vocals are even more impressive when in groups out at sea.

BREEDING
Within their breeding range, pairs normally nest alone. However, Lake Myvatn in Iceland is one such place where they're closer together.

The 'WHEN, WHERE & KEY FACTS'

WHEN TO SEE THEM

Are said to breed farthest north of all the world's duck species. In the UK during winter, but all the time is spent at sea and coastally.

BEST LOCATIONS

Since all their time is spent at sea, the most likely places to see Long-tailed ducks are from any sea-watching points, e.g. the North Sea coastline in England, but even more so in northern Scotland and the islands of Shetland & Orkney.

UK DISTRIBUTION

LIFESPAN ~ 10 YEARS ~

SOCIABILITY ~ FLOCKS ~

SUMMER ~ N/A
WINTER ~ 11,000 individuals

POPULATION STATUS

DUCKLING

THE DUCKS | 77

Mallard

Mallard
Anas platyrhynchos

LEAST CONCERN LC

Did you know?
Apart from the domestic Muscovy duck, the Mallard is the ancestor of all domestic ducks. They are also the most numerous species of duck in the world.

ABOUT

DESCRIPTION
The drake has the iconic metallic green head and bright yellow beak. Most of the body is grey and sandwiched between a brown breast and black rear end. The female is mottled brown with orange-brown beaks. The blue, white-bordered speculum patch on the wing is found on both sexes of Mallard.

BEHAVIOUR
Frequent 'up-enders', feeding on underwater plants. Strong breeding success has been down to their ability to adapt well to human changes. As a result, Mallards have become very tame.

HABITAT
Almost all habitat types as long as conditions are not too severe, which explains their population success. This includes lakes, ponds, urban parks, reservoirs, farms, bogs, & marshes.

VOICE
That unmistakable duck's quack everyone knows is sounded by the female. Males give a quieter 'yeeb' sound.

BREEDING
Mallards generally nest on the ground, close to water & well concealed. They may also nest in more unusual places.

THE DUCKS | 79

The 'WHEN, WHERE & KEY FACTS'

WHEN TO SEE THEM
Resident all year as breeders, but also many migrants from Northern European & Icelandic breeding sites spend winter here.

BEST LOCATIONS
Mallards are the most common and widespread duck species in the world. Wherever there is some form of wetland habitat, it is likely to be home to a Mallard, in both urban and rural settings. Numbers are fewer in the more upland areas.

UK DISTRIBUTION

LIFESPAN ~ 15-25 YEARS ~

SOCIABILITY ~ FLOCKS ~

SUMMER ~ 61,000 - 146,000 pairs
WINTER ~ 710,000 individuals

POPULATION STATUS

DUCKLING

Mandarin

Mandarin
Aix galericulata

LEAST CONCERN
LC

Did you know?

Mandarin populations have never been under threat due to their visual attractiveness for collections. The meat of Mandarins is also known to have an unappealing taste.

ABOUT

DESCRIPTION

Drakes in breeding plumage have the most ornamental appearance of all waterfowl. Its colours include a metallic green-black and glossy crown, tawny brown ruff of feathers on the front and side of neck, and a maroon breast leading to a red beak. Females are mostly grey and dark brown with a white eye ring.

BEHAVIOUR

Mandarins feed on water & land, walking easily. They frequently perch on branches as they are quite shy and can take refuge there.

HABITAT

They avoid open ground, opting for the mature deciduous woodland or parks instead. Present also at small and quiet pools, ponds and streams.

VOICE

The males have a weak whistling call and the ducks a soft quack. Otherwise a very silent duck.

BREEDING

Its natural breeding range is East Asia. In the UK, their nests are often close to captive collections. Either a natural tree hole or a man-made nest box will be the chosen site.

The 'WHEN, WHERE & KEY FACTS'

WHEN TO SEE THEM

Feral populations have formed in the UK through regular captive collection escapes. Mandarins were added to the British list in 1971.

BEST LOCATIONS

The south, eastern and central areas of England host the main populations. However, due to the regular escapees, birds are present in smaller numbers in the north of England, Wales and Scotland too.

UK DISTRIBUTION

LIFESPAN ~ 10 YEARS ~

SOCIABILITY ~ PAIRS ~

SUMMER ~ 2,300 pairs
WINTER ~ 7,000 individuals

POPULATION STATUS

DUCKLING

Pintail

Pintail
Anas acuta

LEAST CONCERN LC

Did you know?

Pintails have a slim body shape and trim form as well as a swift flight. For this reason, they are sometimes referred to as the 'greyhound' of the air.

ABOUT

DESCRIPTION

One of our most iconic & elegant ducks. Males have a coffee-cream head & neck with a narrow white line that extends up from the breast. The rest of the body is a fine wavy-textured grey colour with the long-pointed tail, hence the name. Females are similar in colour to the female Mallard, but slighter built & more graceful.

BEHAVIOUR

Pintails demonstrate typical dabbling duck behaviour, feeding on the water surface and upending. They are at ease on land, grazing occasionally & mix well with other species.

HABITAT

Breeding takes place in shallow freshwater lakes mainly in Europe and coastal areas in winter.

VOICE

The drake has a high-pitched & melodious whistle, often double-noted. Females have a low, prolonged quack.

BREEDING

The nests are loosely constructed from dry vegetation and less concealed than those of most other ducks. Drakes are also present during early fledging; unlike most ducks.

THE DUCKS | 85

The 'WHEN, WHERE & KEY FACTS'

WHEN TO SEE THEM
Resident all year, however a lot more birds arrive in September from mainland Europe to over-winter here until around March.

BEST LOCATIONS
Due to their preference for shallow & sheltered waters, locations such as the Solway Firth Estuary, Dee Estuary and Ouse Washes play host to a large number of Pintails throughout the winter.

UK DISTRIBUTION

~ LIFESPAN ~ 15-25 YEARS ~

~ SOCIABILITY ~ FLOCKS ~

SUMMER ~ 9-33 pairs
WINTER ~ 29,000 individuals

POPULATION STATUS

DUCKLING

86 | THE DUCKS

Pochard

Pochard
Aythya ferina

LEAST CONCERN LC

ABOUT

Did you know?

Pochards form some of the largest flock of ducks during the winter. They often group together with other diving ducks such as Tufted ducks which they are also known to hybridise with.

DESCRIPTION

The head & upper neck of male Pochards is a rich chestnut with a medium grey body and wings to contrast. On closer view, a fine dark brown texture is seen (vermiculation). Breast and rear are jet black. Females are a brownish colour with a mottled appearance around the neck and breast area. They also have a white line through & around the area of the eye.

BEHAVIOUR

Most time is spent on the water due to their awkwardness on land. They dive for food in shallow areas, upending or dabbling. Very sociable outside breeding season.

HABITAT

For breeding, lakes, ponds & slow-flowing streams that are well vegetated. At other times, sheltered bays and river estuaries.

VOICE

Males are mostly silent with a wheezy-like call sounded at times. During display, a harsh 'kurr' comes by the females.

BREEDING

Thick vegetation on or near to ponds or lakes. It is common for two ducks, particularly the Tufted duck, to lay in the same nest as the Pochard duck.

The 'WHEN, WHERE & KEY FACTS'

WHEN TO SEE THEM
Mostly seen in UK during autumn and winter; large numbers come from Eastern Europe and Russia. Not common breeders in the UK.

BEST LOCATIONS
In summer, open lakes and gravel pits in lowland eastern England and Scotland. In the winter, they can be found throughout the UK, on large lakes, estuaries and the sheltered coastal bays.

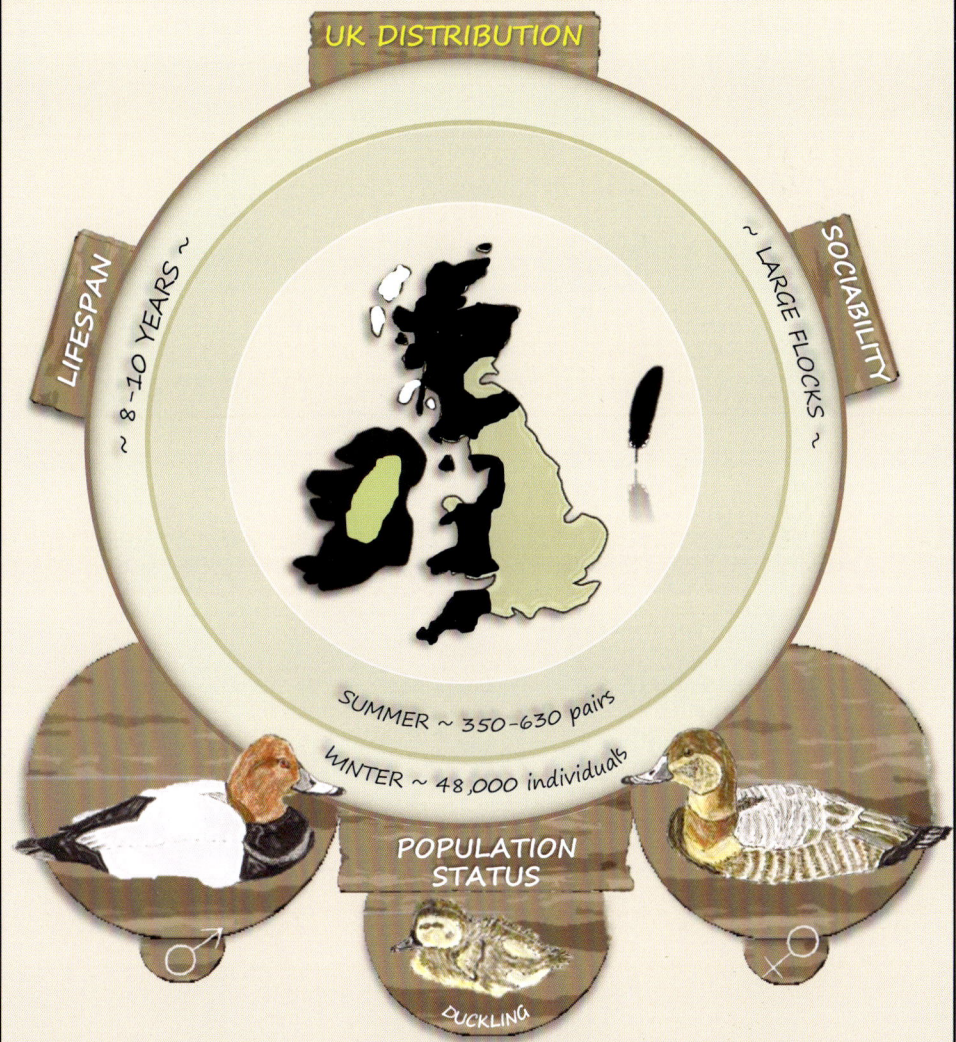

UK DISTRIBUTION

LIFESPAN ~ 8-10 YEARS ~

SOCIABILITY ~ LARGE FLOCKS ~

SUMMER ~ 350-630 pairs
WINTER ~ 48,000 individuals

POPULATION STATUS

DUCKLING

Red-breasted Merganser

90 | THE DUCKS

Red-breasted Merganser
Mergus serrator

LEAST CONCERN LC

Did you know?

Five species of merganser exist across the world; Red-breasted Mergansers are the most widespread of all. 'Merganser' comes from the Latin, roughly translating to 'plunging goose'.

ABOUT

DESCRIPTION

Breeding drakes have a long shaggy crest with a dark bottle-green head & black stripe down the nape. Upper breast is brown spotted, more of which is found on the females. Duck is like the Goosander with a rufous brown head and neck. Upperparts are dark grey-brown; crest is shorter than males. Both sexes have ruby-red beak with black culmen & spiked crest.

BEHAVIOUR

Often seen pattering across the water upon take-off; recorded at flying of speeds up to 80mph. Very skilled divers with serrated beaks that enhances their ability to grasp slippery fish prey.

HABITAT

Inland waters such as lakes and rivers during breeding. Outside this time, they spend more time on the shallower coastal waters. More maritime than the related Goosander.

VOICE

A mostly silent duck. During the courtship display, males utter a mewing sound and females a 'krrr' noise.

BREEDING

Unlike other members of this genus, dense scrub near water is chosen over tree holes.

The 'WHEN, WHERE & KEY FACTS'

WHEN TO SEE THEM

Numbers reach a peak in December when birds flock on the coast having arrived from their north European breeding grounds.

BEST LOCATIONS

The north-west of England, Wales, Scotland and areas of N. Ireland host most breeding birds. Wintering sites include the north Norfolk coast; Morecambe Bay, Lancashire; Exe Estuary, Devon; Culbin sands in n. Scotland & Belfast Lough.

UK DISTRIBUTION

LIFESPAN ~ 8 YEARS ~

SOCIABILITY ~ LARGE FLOCKS ~

SUMMER ~ 2,400 pairs

WINTER ~ 9,000 individuals

POPULATION STATUS

♂   DUCKLING   ♀

92 | THE DUCKS

Ruddy Duck

Ruddy Duck
Oxyura jamaicensis

LEAST CONCERN
LC

Did you know?
Ruddy ducks lay eggs that are not only big, white and pebbly textured but are also the largest of all ducks relative to their body size. Males cock their tails during courtship display, hence their other name 'stifftail'.

ABOUT

DESCRIPTION
Ruddy ducks are small and compact with a cartoon-style look, characterised by a broad, scoop-shaped beak & fanned stiff tail. Males have unique bright blue beaks, jet-black head and white cheeks. Rest of body is chestnut brown. Females are paler brown and lightly barred. A dark stripe also runs across a pale cheek.

BEHAVIOUR
Mostly water based due to their large & far set back feet. Ruddy ducks regularly dive to catch invertebrates such as midge larvae, molluscs and water-beetles.

HABITAT
Reservoirs & large lakes are preferred during the winter. Reedy ponds & gravel pits are used during breeding.

VOICE
Almost entirely silent. A frog-like croak is sounded by males during the courtship displays. The female has a low nasal call to gather her brood.

BREEDING
Quite a secretive bird during breeding. Tall reed beds are usually chosen with piles of vegetation used as the structure for the nest.

The 'WHEN, WHERE & KEY FACTS'

WHEN TO SEE THEM

Since 1999, the UK Government has led the eradication of the Ruddy duck. There are now thought to be less than 100 birds left, but resident here all year.

BEST LOCATIONS

The remaining populations of Ruddy ducks are mainly found in the West Midlands, northern parts of England, Anglesey and southern Scotland. Large lakes & reservoirs are favoured places.

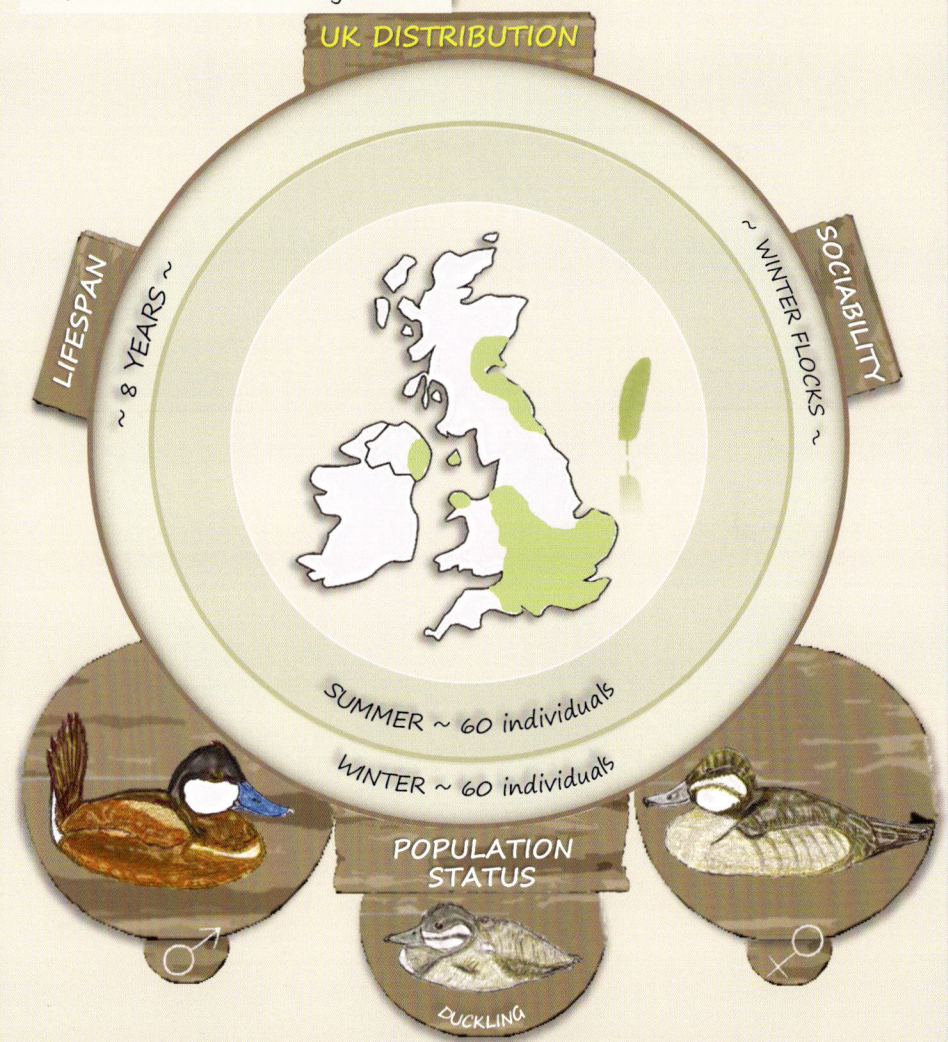

UK DISTRIBUTION

LIFESPAN ~ 8 YEARS ~

SOCIABILITY ~ WINTER FLOCKS ~

SUMMER ~ 60 individuals
WINTER ~ 60 individuals

POPULATION STATUS

DUCKLING

Scaup
Aythya marila

LEAST CONCERN LC

Did you know?
Two look-alike species make up the Scaup superspecies. The Lesser Scaup is found only in North America, the Greater Scaup across Eurasia & North America and is the species that occurs in the UK.

ABOUT

DESCRIPTION
One of the larger diving ducks. Males have glossy green-black heads with white bellies and flanks. Their tail, neck & breast are black. The back is textured in grey and black. Female plumage shows various shades of brown. The head and back are darker, but the breast & flanks are pale buff. They also have a white patch at the base of the bill. Both sexes have bluish beaks.

BEHAVIOUR
Very gregarious birds especially through the winter. Large 'rafts' collect mainly on coastal salt waters; providing good depths for diving.

VOICE
Mainly a silent bird. During the courtship display the male utters a soft whistle to which the female responds with a low-pitched 'krr'.

HABITAT
Scaup seek the shelter of coastal bays & estuaries when visiting the UK in the winter. They also inhabit unfrozen fresh water along the coast where diving is possible.

BREEDING
Birds arrive here for winter having bred in Iceland & Northern Europe. A handful only breed in the UK, hence it is our rarest breeding species of waterfowl.

The 'WHEN, WHERE & KEY FACTS'

WHEN TO SEE THEM

Arrive in the late October from their Icelandic and Northern European breeding grounds. They return again in March.

BEST LOCATIONS

Greater Scaup colonies gather round most parts of the UK's coastlines in winter, including estuaries e.g. the Dee in Merseyside, Forth & Moray (Firths) of Scotland and the Solway that forms part of the border between England and Scotland.

UK DISTRIBUTION

~ LIFESPAN ~ 10-12 YEARS ~

~ SOCIABILITY ~ LARGE FLOCKS ~

SUMMER ~ Up to 5 pairs
WINTER ~ 12,000 individuals

POPULATION STATUS

DUCKLING

98 | THE DUCKS

SHELDUCK

Shelduck
Tadorna tadorna

LEAST CONCERN LC

ABOUT

Did you know?
Unlike most other ducks, pairs of Shelduck maintain bonds for several years. They are the only species that feed by walking forward with their bill submerged just beneath the mudflats, called scything.

DESCRIPTION
The UK's biggest duck; larger than a Mallard, smaller than a goose. Drakes have a sharply defined, glossy, dark green head and upper neck. Most of the rest of the body is crisp white with a broad chestnut band at the breast. Females are alike in their colour patterning (monomorphism), only a little duller & smaller. Bill of male is brighter red with a knob at base.

BEHAVIOUR
Having some goose-like characteristics, such as the time spent out of water grazing. Shelducks are gregarious but also territorial when breeding.

HABITAT
Shelducks prefer saline (saltwater) habitats & therefore frequent mud flats and muddy or sandy estuaries. Fresh-water habitats are used for drinking purposes.

VOICE
Relatively silent outside breeding. Males become noisy when in larger numbers, sounding a low whistle & a variety of squawks. Females have a harsh barking quack.

BREEDING
Nests are usually found in rabbit burrows but also tree-hollows above ground, less often will nests be in the open or amongst vegetation.

The 'WHEN, WHERE & KEY FACTS'

WHEN TO SEE THEM
Resident throughout the year with numbers reaching their peak during the winter period.

BEST LOCATIONS
Found on almost all coastal areas around the British Isles, but less so in western N. Ireland & Scotland. They can also be found on inland waters, including reservoirs and gravel pits, for drinking fresh water.

UK DISTRIBUTION

LIFESPAN ~ 5-15 YEARS ~

SOCIABILITY ~ PAIRS & SMALL FLOCKS ~

SUMMER ~ 15,000 pairs
WINTER ~ 61,000 individuals

POPULATION STATUS

DUCKLING

THE DUCKS | 101

SHOVELER

102 | THE DUCKS

Shoveler
Anas clypeata

LEAST CONCERN LC

Did you know?
Often referred to as the spoonbill due to their large & unique spatulate beaks. These beaks have over 100 fine lamellae for straining small animals, insects and plant matter from the mud & water.

ABOUT

DESCRIPTION
The drake in breeding plumage has a metallic green head. Their lower neck and breast is white leading round to the cinnamon-chestnut brown flanks. A green speculum is bordered with white. Female Shovelers are mottled in many brown & buff shades like the Mallard. Both sexes have the unique spatulate beaks with comb-like projections.

BEHAVIOUR
Usually occurs in small groups of up to twenty. One of the busiest of dabblers, using their large spoon-like beaks to sift the mud & water for nutrients and insects.

VOICE
Due to the time spent working away in the water, Shovelers are very quiet. Males have a low double-noted 'tok tok' whilst ducks sound a hoarse quack.

HABITAT
Breeds by shallow pools, meres & marshes with good cover. During the winter, flooded ground, freshwater marsh but not often salt water.

BREEDING
The nests are most often found close to water, on dry ground and fairly open sites. Both sexes bob their heads during courtship.

THE DUCKS | 103

The 'WHEN, WHERE & KEY FACTS'

WHEN TO SEE THEM

Resident in the UK all year round. Yet, in large areas of Wales, north-west N. Ireland, east N. Ireland and the south-west of England most birds overwinter rather than breed.

BEST LOCATIONS

The UK supports more than 20% of the N-W European Shoveler population. Many more are here in the winter, especially in S & E England, e.g. Ouse Washes, Rutland waters & the Herts. & Middlesex WT reserves of Tring, Amwell & Stocker's Lake. Some occur in Scotland and parts of W. England.

UK DISTRIBUTION

~ LIFESPAN ~ 10–20 YEARS ~

~ SOCIABILITY ~ SMALL FLOCKS ~

SUMMER ~ Up to 1,020 pairs
WINTER ~ 18,000 individuals

POPULATION STATUS

DUCKLING

104 | THE DUCKS

Smew

Smew
Mergus albellus

LEAST CONCERN
LC

ABOUT

Did you know?
The smallest species in the Mergus genus, which includes the Goosander and Red-breasted Merganser. Also treated as belonging to another genus, Mergellus, and is the only living member.

DESCRIPTION
Unmistakable for any other duck. The male Smew is almost entirely white in his breeding plumage, with a black patch around the eye, beak and on the crest. Females are chestnut brown on head & back of neck. Their cheeks are also white & the rest of the upperparts are mottled in a medium grey. Both sexes have greenish-grey-coloured beaks.

BEHAVIOUR
Unlike the larger Merganser, Smew tend to opt for the smaller & shallower waters. They swim, dive & walk with ease, often perching on branches in woodlands.

HABITAT
The few Smew that do winter in the UK are most likely to inhabit the smaller lakes, ponds, rivers & estuaries; usually in less wooded areas.

VOICE
Vocalise infrequently, except during display. Males give out a dull squeaking call, which is followed up with a hiccup-like noise. Ducks have a hoarse quack.

BREEDING
Smew breed mainly across Siberia. They use tree holes of disused woodpecker nests, natural cavities and man-made boxes.

The 'WHEN, WHERE & KEY FACTS'

WHEN TO SEE THEM
Between December & March when birds move down from their Siberian breeding grounds. Some will come across from Denmark & Holland if freezing conditions hit those parts.

BEST LOCATIONS
Smew will occasionally appear on smaller areas of water. They tend to be found in the South-East & West of the UK. Recordings include the Ouse Washes in Cambridgeshire, Rutland Waters, Rye Harbour in East Sussex and Amwell in Hertfordshire.

UK DISTRIBUTION

LIFESPAN ~ 8 YEARS ~

SOCIABILITY ~ FLOCKS ~

SUMMER ~ n/a
WINTER ~ Up to 180 individuals

POPULATION STATUS

DUCKLING

Teal

Teal
Anas crecca

LEAST CONCERN LC

Did you know?
The smallest wild duck to occur in the UK. The American and Eurasian forms of the 'Green-winged' Teal are still considered different species by many due to a couple of differences in plumage pattern.

ABOUT

DESCRIPTION
The smallest duck to occur in the UK & indeed the world. Males have a rich chestnut brown head & neck. A mask-like, glossy bottle green runs from the eye to the base of neck. The body is patterned finely pale grey & black, with a white band above where the wings lie. Females have the typical buff and brown-mottled colour, with a dark crown on top.

BEHAVIOUR
Very agile ducks due to their small size; able to take off from a static position. Normally feed at night or dusk when disturbance is unlikely.

HABITAT
For breeding, pools or lakes with plenty of vegetation is preferred; marshes and peat bogs too. Winter likewise, but with the addition of estuaries and mudflats.

VOICE
Both sexes have high pitched voices. Males give off a single-noted whistle whilst females a fast-paced quack.

BREEDING
Teal prefer shallow waters at breeding times, with woodland nearby. Like Mallards, multiple males will display to a single female, often followed with a chase.

THE DUCKS | 109

The 'WHEN, WHERE & KEY FACTS'

WHEN TO SEE THEM

All year round, but many more arrive in winter to the south & west of the UK, often from continental Europe, particularly the Baltics & Siberia, to escape the harsher winters there.

BEST LOCATIONS

Inland & coastal wetlands support many in winter, with important sites around the Somerset Levels and Mersey Estuary near Liverpool. Others include WT reserves e.g. East Chevington in Northumberland, Thurrock Tameside in Essex, Wheldrake Ings in Yorkshire and Pwllpatti in Powys.

UK DISTRIBUTION

~ LIFESPAN ~ 10-15 YEARS ~

~ SOCIABILITY ~ SMALL FLOCKS ~

SUMMER ~ Up to 2,800 pairs
WINTER ~ 220,000 individuals

POPULATION STATUS

DUCKLING

TUFTED DUCK

Tufted Duck
Aythya fulingula

LEAST CONCERN LC

ABOUT

Did you know?

An 'Old World' bird, which is the European counterpart of the North American Ring-Necked duck. Tufteds have a tuft of hair or pony-tail, but lack the white band at the base of the bill.

DESCRIPTION

Tufteds are a medium-sized diving duck with males mostly black and having a purple gloss around the head. Their upperparts also appear black but have a green gloss. Flanks are white in contrast. Females are dark brown with paler sides. Both sexes share a crest or pony-tail, but the male's is longer down the neck. Both have yellow eyes & bluish grey beak.

BEHAVIOUR

Except during periods of hard frost, Tufteds are rare on the sea. Small flocks gather on reservoirs, ponds and lakes where they are seen to dive frequently below water for food.

HABITAT

Fresh waters of varying size, especially those with reed beds & other aquatic plants providing roots, seeds & insects.

VOICE

Not a very vocal duck. Males sound a soft repeating whistle. The female has the typical diving duck 'kurr kurr'.

BREEDING

Nests are always near to the water, hidden under reeds or bushes. If islands are available these will often be used. Otherwise, the bank of a pool, pond or small lake are usually chosen.

The 'WHEN, WHERE & KEY FACTS'

WHEN TO SEE THEM

In the UK all year round. Numbers increase significantly in the winter as further birds arrive from Iceland and N. Europe. About our 4th most numerous duck during the winter.

BEST LOCATIONS

Breeds in most lowland areas of the UK, but less frequently in Wales and the south-west of England, e.g. Devon & Cornwall. Everywhere in winter though, except the Scottish Highlands. Lakes, ponds and reservoirs are always likely places.

UK DISTRIBUTION

~ LIFESPAN ~ 10-15 YEARS ~

~ SOCIABILITY ~ SMALL FLOCKS ~

SUMMER ~ 19,000 pairs
WINTER ~ 110,000 individuals

POPULATION STATUS

DUCKLING

THE DUCKS | 113

Velvet Scoter

Velvet Scoter
Melanitta fusca

VULNERABLE — VU

Did you know?
The largest of the scoter species that occur in the UK and worldwide. Those from East Siberia and North America are named the White-winged Scoter, considered by many to be a separate species.

ABOUT

DESCRIPTION
A little larger than the Common Scoter. Apart from the white eye and wing patches, the male is entirely black. They have an orange beak with a black knob at the base and legs are a red-orange. Ducks are dark brown with a buff patch on the lores (area between eye and beak) and ear coverts. The beak is slate-grey without the knob. Legs are also duller orange.

BEHAVIOUR
Regular divers, feeding primarily on molluscs, which includes clams & mussels. Gather into small groups on the sea during winter in the UK.

HABITAT
At sea in the winter in the UK. They like sandy seabeds to feed on sand eels and exposed ocean to dive for shellfish, small fish etc., sheltered bays on occasion too.

VOICE
Generally silent outside breeding. During courtship males sound a bell-like and croaking call, females a thin whistle.

BREEDING
Velvet Scoter do not breed in the UK, even though small numbers sometimes appear in summer. For breeding, inland waters such as lakes, pools, and rivers are chosen.

The 'WHEN, WHERE & KEY FACTS'

WHEN TO SEE THEM

Migrating south from Siberian and Scandinavian breeding grounds in the Autumn to overwinter in the UK. Numbers start to fall again as birds return north in early Spring.

BEST LOCATIONS

Small groups are found along the North Sea coast & often mix with Common Scoters; but generally more northerly distributed. Flocks of around 50 birds are typical from Norfolk up towards the eastern Scottish firths and sheltered bays.

UK DISTRIBUTION

LIFESPAN ~ 10-12 YEARS ~

SOCIABILITY ~ FLOCKS ~

SUMMER ~ n/a
WINTER ~ 2,500 individuals

POPULATION STATUS

DUCKLING

116 | THE DUCKS

Wigeon

♂

♀

THE DUCKS | 117

Wigeon
Anas penelope

LEAST CONCERN
LC

ABOUT

Did you know?

An unorthodox method of feeding, spending much of their time grazing on land like a goose. Wigeon also have a reputation for snatching food from diving ducks when they resurface.

DESCRIPTION

A medium-large species of dabbling duck. Breeding males have rufous-coloured heads with a buff-yellow crown and forehead. The breast is a pinkish colour, the rest of the body is a finely textured blue-grey. The females are orange washed grey-brown on their upperparts with strong mottling and speckling on the head. Both sexes have a pale blue bill with black nail.

BEHAVIOUR

Wigeon usually stay in small groups on their own. They are the duck version of a goose with much time spent out of the water grazing.

HABITAT

Small lakes and pools as well as bracken slopes & moorland tarns during breeding. In the winter, dense flocks gather on shallow coastal waters, estuaries & inland lakes.

VOICE

Males emit a simple "whee-OOO" whistle. In contrast, females give off a growling sound or low purring.

BREEDING

Ground nesting, most often in thick waterside vegetation or under low-lying bushes. Males are known to re-join the family when the mother takes the ducklings to water.

The 'WHEN, WHERE & KEY FACTS'

WHEN TO SEE THEM

All year round, many more during the winter. Our next most populous duck after the Mallard. In the winter, birds come to the UK from Iceland, Scandinavia and Russia.

BEST LOCATIONS

In winter, large numbers of Wigeon are found around the coast. Some of the best places to see dense flocks are the Ouse Washes, Cambridgeshire, the Montrose Basin in Angus, East Chevington in Northumberland, Pwllpatti in Powys and Wheldrake Ings in Yorkshire.

UK DISTRIBUTION

~ LIFESPAN ~ 15 YEARS ~

~ DENSE FLOCKS ~ SOCIABILITY ~

SUMMER ~ 300-500 pairs
WINTER ~ 450,000 individuals

POPULATION STATUS

DUCKLING

THE DUCKS | 119

OTHER VISITORS

The list of species officially recorded in Great Britain is maintained by the British Ornithologists' Union. Birds are placed into certain categories depending on the nature of their occurrence in the UK. Due to the location of the British Isles, a number of ducks & geese occasionally turn up on their migration from Asia & North America. Each of the birds illustrated here are included on the British list as vagrants, not as residents.

Surf Scoter

A dark form of Snow goose also exists, known as the 'Blue-phase' Snow goose.

Snow goose

Barrow's Goldeneye

The American Wigeon is the New World counterpart of the Eurasian Wigeon.

Steller's Eider

Ring-necked duck

Black duck

Redhead

Cackling goose

American Wigeon

Hooded Merganser

Up until 2004, the Cackling goose was a sub-species of the Canada goose, but is now classed as a separate species.

Blue-winged Teal

NOT ONE OF THESE?

At times, you may observe a duck or even a goose that neither looks or sounds familiar and doesn't feature in any of your field guides and identification books. Unlike the songbirds that dart from tree to tree and in and out of bushes or hedgerows, waterfowl are comparatively much easier to watch. The patterning and distinctiveness of their plumage — males more so than females between species — also makes for easier identification. Therefore, if you see a bird that doesn't match any in this book or another on waterfowl bear in mind the following.

1. **It's a domestic duck**

   Likely to be the most common answer, since most guides about waterfowl do not include the domestic varieties. Usually found in parks, domestic ducks & geese spend more time on land than their wild counterparts. They are also more relaxed around people, having been reared and kept in captivity as a source of eggs & meat for perhaps hundreds of years.

2. **It's an exotic duck**

   Ducks and geese will sometimes join other flocks of birds when undertaking migration journeys or perhaps unintentionally take a different route when weather conditions are severe. More frequently they will be found in the wild after having escaped from a private captive collection.

3. **It's a hybrid duck**

   The result of two distant species such as Goldeneye & Red-breasted Merganser breeding together. Most common where birds are kept together in captivity. Birds show features from both parent species.

4. **It's in eclipse plumage**

   Male ducks go through a transition where their plumage turns duller over the summer, closely resembling their female partners.

ORGANISATIONS

The Wildfowl & Wetlands Trust (WWT) is one of the world's largest and most respected conservation organisations. The Trust works globally to safeguard and improve wetlands, not only for their wildlife inhabitants but also for the people who rely and work in and around them.

The Trust was founded in 1946 by the late Sir Peter Scott at its HQ, Slimbridge in Gloucestershire. The WWT complement their conservation work carried out worldwide with a network of nine visitor centres across the UK. These consist of globally important wetland habitats that cater for the numerous captive-held species of waterfowl but also visiting birds from the UK and overseas.

The Royal Society for the Protection of Birds (RSPB) was founded in 1889 to help prevent the trade of plumes (a bird's display feathers). These were used to make women's hats, causing the severe decline of birds like Egrets and some Birds of Paradise species.

With the organisation's success in its early years, the RSPB was granted the Royal Charter 15 years after establishment. It is now Europe's largest wildlife conservation organisation with over 1 million members. The Society's activities are focussed on species and habitats in greatest need. The RSPB runs campaigns besides manging over 200 reserves and is the UK's official Birdlife International partner, a global collaboration of nature conservation organisations.

The Wildlife Trusts began life as the Society for the Promotion of Nature Reserves (SPNR) formed by Charles Rothschild in 1912. The first independent trust was in Norfolk; this was slowly followed by the formation of other trusts that soon spread nationwide.

The early trusts tended to focus on the purchase of land to grow their network of reserves, with these independent trusts eventually forming one federation, today known as the Wildlife Trusts. The organisation is made up of 47 local trusts in the UK, Isle of Man and Alderney (one of the Channel Islands), with the Royal Society of Wildlife Trusts acting as the umbrella organisation. There are over 2,300 locations to visit, covering 95,000 hectares of land.

The British Trust for Ornithology (BTO) was founded by Max Nicholson in 1933 with the aim of studying the birds of the British Isles. The BTO's work ensures that we continue to improve our knowledge and understanding about Britain's bird populations.

The BTO is an independent charitable research institute that combines professional and citizen science with the evidence of wildlife population changes used by Government and non-governmental organisation (NGO) campaigners. The information is gathered by over 40,000 volunteer birdwatchers about the status of UK birds, which sets a standard across the globe to better understand the effects of environmental shifts and the cost of this to our wildlife.

The International Wild Waterfowl Association (IWWA) is a non-Governmental organisation established in 1958 by a small group of aviculturists, including Sir Peter Scott, who had the awareness and vision to realise both the ongoing as well as future problems facing waterfowl.

The IWWA has multiple different causes to which it is committed to, such as protecting & enhancing waterfowl habitats, supporting captive breeding of endangered species and conservation project partnerships. Today, the IWWA consists of private aviculturists, students, conservationists, zoo professionals, general waterfowl enthusiasts, researchers and many others from around the world focussed on preserving waterfowl in the wild.

The British Waterfowl Association (BWA) is a charity and association of waterfowl enthusiasts interested in the keeping, breeding and conservation of both wild and domestic waterfowl. The charity is also concerned with educating people about waterfowl and the importance of learning to conserve and protect such birds.

The BWA aims to teach present and future generations about the importance of breeding and safeguarding wildfowl. In addition, it also promotes the requirement for an increase in the standards for those who keep and breed any ducks, geese or swans in captivity, to ensure a prosperous future for all waterfowl. Members of the BWA are also invited to advertise birds for sale.

GLOSSARY OF 'FOWL' TERMS

ANATINAE ~ the sub-family of the overarching Anatidae family. Contains all the ducks of the dabbling duck tribe.

ANATIDAE ~ the over-arching biological family of birds that includes the ducks, geese and swans. They occur on all the continents except for Antarctica.

BOG ~ a wet and spongy, badly drained peaty soil, usually acid and mainly composed of moss & heath.

ALTRICIAL ~ describes a newly hatched bird (or animal), perhaps blind, unable to move or feed itself alone, that requires care and feeding by the parents for a longer period of time to survive.

ANSERIFORMES ~ an order of birds comprised of three families and around 180 species. The largest family is the Anatidae, with over 170 species of waterfowl.

AQUATIC ~ birds or animals that live on or near to water as their principal habitat. A more aquatic duck is one that spends more of its time on the water.

CRUSTACEANS ~ a large group of arthropods, characterised by their segmented bodies and paired limbs e.g. crabs & shrimps. The diets of Waterfowl consist of these smaller water dwellers.

DABBLE ~ to feed on the surface of the water, often with a skimming action.

DOWN ~ the soft and finest feathers found underneath the tough exterior feathers of adult birds. They help to insulate the birds and its nest, and aid buoyancy.

EUTROPHIC ~ those waters rich in mineral and organic nutrients that promote the growth of plant life, especially algae.

FEN ~ An alkaline body of water supplied by surface & ground water mainly.

FERAL ~ a bird that has returned to a wild state after being kept captive, but has escaped & then established its own self-sustaining wild population.

ESTUARY ~ the wide part of a river at the place where it meets the sea.

FLEDGE ~ a young bird which develops flight feathers in order to leave the nest.

FRESHWATER ~ non-salty water of inland watercourses.

GANDER ~ name of the male goose.

GENUS ~ the major sub-division of a family or subfamily that often consists of multiple species.

GIZZARD ~ the muscular and thick-walled part of a bird's stomach used for grinding food.

GOOSE ~ name of the female goose.

GOSLING ~ a young goose.

HYBRID ~ an offspring produced from two birds of different species breeding together.

IMMATURE ~ a bird that has gone through its first moult (out of juvenile plumage), but hasn't yet reached the breeding age & fully developed its adult feathers.

JUVENILE ~ a young bird just fledged and so in its first flying stage, but still retaining most of its downy feathers worn whilst in the nest.

MANDIBLE ~ the upper or lower parts of a beak.

LAMELLAE ~ the thin plate-like tissue structure found on the edges of a waterfowl's beak. These look like teeth, acting as sieves to filter the water and to tear of plant stems.

MARSH ~ soft, wet & low-lying habitat characterised by grassy vegetation. Often an area between water and firmer ground.

MONOGAMOUS ~ having one mate through the breeding season. Some birds – particularly swans – will form bonds for several years until one dies.

MOULT ~ to shed the feathers as part of the annual life cycle.

MOLLUSCS ~ invertebrates such as snails, slugs and mussels that have soft and unsegmented bodies. They live mainly in marine habitats, but also fresh-water and even terrestrial.

PRECOCIAL ~ the opposite of 'Altricial'. The newly born able to move freely and therefore require little or no care by the parents to survive.

TRIBE ~ a taxonomic rank below family.

SEDENTARY ~ birds that stay in one area & do not migrate to a different area or country on season change.

TUNDRA ~ treeless plains in the arctic region of Europe, Asia, & N. America where the subsoil is permanently frozen and the land is typically flat.

PLACES TO VISIT

TOP SITES FOR WINTERING WATERFOWL

A. The Wash
B. Wallasea Wetlands
C. East Chevington
D. Ribble Estuary
E. Morecambe Bay
F. N. Norfolk Coast
G. Thames Estuary
H. Humber Estuary
I. Dee Estuary
J. Somerset Levels
K. Solway Estuary
L. Strangford Lough
M. Firth of Forth
N. Firth of Clyde
O. Wexford Slobs
P. Lough Neagh
Q. Shannon Callows

THE WILDFOWL & WETLANDS TRUST

Each centre has its own resident collection of waterfowl which include both UK national birds as well as many other species from around the world. In fact, the WWT helps both wildlife and people in 77 countries globally. This involves restoring wetland habitats and promoting sustainable livelihoods as well as monitoring the birds' populations connecting the two.

The extensive grounds and mosaic of pools are managed by the trust with significant support from over 200,000 members, donations towards global spanning projects, and hands-on work by volunteers. Each centre hosts a gift shop, restaurant, and activity & function rooms; all with disabled access. Regular talks and feeds are provided by centre staff with other activities such as floodlit swan feeds scheduled through the seasons.

ARUNDEL ~ Mill Road, Arundel, West Sussex, BN18 9PB

Arundel hosts a haven of reedbeds, ponds and meadows that support an abundance of wetland wildlife. The paved pathways lead round the international wildfowl collections, including Nene geese & Black-necked swans. An SSSI (Site of Special Scientific Interest) boardwalk, one of the largest in Sussex, leads through dense reeds where water rails, warblers and bitterns may be spotted. A boat safari also travels through the wet meadow and reedbeds with the chance of seeing water voles crunching on reed shoots.

CAERLAVEROCK ~ Eastpark Farm, Dumfriesshire, DG1 4RS

Most northerly of the WWT's centres, Caerlaverock plays host to an amazing winter spectacle of many thousand geese, ducks, and swans that flock here to feed beneath the Solway skies. These include Barnacle geese from Svalbard and Whooper swans from October until April. Come summer, the open coastal scenery sees Osprey fishing on the tide, having nested here each year since 2006. The centre's wetlands can be explored from a series of hides and secluded avenues that provide a closer encounter with the birds.

CASTLE ESPIE ~ Comber, Newtownards, Co. Down, BT23 6EA

Found on the very attractive shores of Britain's largest inlet that is Strangford Lough in eastern Northern Ireland. Castle Espie offers a mix of tidal lagoons, woodland walks, eel-grass mats, salt marshes and many more wetland habitats. Such diversity of habitats also brings a similar variety of wildlife, including the Light-bellied race of Brent goose between October and March, as well as waders such as Redshank and Curlew. Castle Espie also hosts the largest collection of rare and exotic water birds in Ireland.

LLANELLI ~ Llwynhendy, Llanelli, Carmarthenshire, SA14 9SH

The National Wetlands Centre Wales, as it's also known, is set amongst a 450-acre mosaic of lakes, pools, scrapes, streams & lagoons adjoining salt marshes and the scenic Burry Inlet. Thousands of migratory wetland birds, including Shelduck, Shoveler, Black & Bar-tailed Godwit and Snipe visit in the winter. Cycling or even canoeing during the warmer months are alternative ways to explore the collection. There is an increasing population of Little egrets that are often in view, as well as a thriving water vole colony.

LONDON ~ Queen Elizabeth's Walk, Barnes, London, SW13 9WT

London Wetland Centre is an oasis situated just ten minutes from the busy commuter district of Hammersmith. This 105-acre nature reserve features a series of pools, lagoons, reedbeds, marshes and meadows, providing a haven for hundreds of wetland creatures. During the winter months, the reedbeds of WWT London are home to the rare Bittern, whilst during the summer evenings, bat walks are provided by the trust.

MARTIN MERE ~ Burscough, Ormskirk, Lancashire, L40 0TA

Martin Mere is a Ramsar-rated marshland providing a winter sanctuary for large migrating flocks of pink-footed geese that breed in eastern Greenland, Iceland and the Svalbard islands. Thousands of wintering Whooper swans can also be seen at the award-winning 'swan spectacular' between October & March as well as huge migration flocks of Wigeon. Other attractions include the otter enclosure, pond dipping zone and an extensive eco-garden surrounded by around 100 international resident waterbirds.

SLIMBRIDGE ~ Slimbridge, Gloucestershire, GL2 7BT *HQ

The founding centre opened by Sir Peter Scott in November 1946. An early success story for Slimbridge was in the 1950s, saving the Nene goose from extinction. The reserve covers over 800 acres reaching the shores of the Severn estuary protected by a number of international treaties. Canoe hire and a Land Rover safari are alternative ways to explore the grounds during the summer. The Sloane Observation Tower provides views towards the Cotswold Edge escarpment to the east one way and the River Severn and Forest of Dean the other. Bewick's swans are a feature in the winter, arriving from the extreme cold of northern Russia.

WASHINGTON ~ District 15, Wash., Tyne & Wear, NE38 8LE

Washington has 110 acres of diverse wetland, woodland and wildlife. Some of its most notable wildlife within the centre includes a flock of Chilean flamingos besides a great range of ducks, geese and swans. Outside the grounds of the centre there is a nature reserve on the banks of the River Wear. The site's newest habitat - a saline lagoon - floods at high tides to five metres and more, and visited by roe deer and wild otter.

WELNEY ~ Hundred Foot Bank, Nr. Wisbech, Norfolk, PE14 9TN

Set in the rich Fenland landscape, the wetlands at Welney on the Ouse washes is home to some of the most spectacular winter gatherings of swans — the Bewick's and Whooper swans from Arctic Russia and Iceland, respectively. Summer brings a wealth of rare waders and many other types of wildlife. These can be viewed from the secrecy of six different hides around the reserve whilst also gaining different perspectives of the fens habitat.

WWT CONSERVATION WORK

Pioneered by Sir Peter Scott since establishing the WWT in 1946, the trust has been working with local communities in the UK and across the world. In 1962, the first Nene goose was released back into the wild in Hawaii after being reared at Slimbridge. From just 30 individuals, their world population now totals over 2,000. These next two pages demonstrate the extensive scientific research, monitoring programmes and conservation projects the WWT has led for more than 60 years. The WWT's work becomes even more important as pressure grows on the world's wetlands that remain.

~ MISSION MADAGASCAR ~

In the latter half of the 20th century, approximately 60% of Madagascar's wetlands were lost. Until recently, the Madagascar Pochard was thought to be extinct, last sighted in 1991. However, in 2006, a small number of birds were discovered on a single small wetland – Red lake – which soon led to the WWT establishing a captive breeding programme against imminent extinction. The long-term aim is to restore the Pochard to a number of areas it used to inhabit by re-introducing captive-bred birds. With 75 birds at the breeding facility, the world population has nearly quadrupled. Lake Sofia has since been identified as the site to re-release birds and develop a co-management system with villagers.

~ INSPIRING GENERATIONS ~

The WWT has been inspiring generations ever since its foundation. Through the provision of unique outdoor learning environments, these have helped both young and old to make sense of the natural world. After all, people are unlikely to protect something they don't understand the purpose, value and effect of on our daily lives.

With funding from HSBC, the WWT has provided a free learning experience to thousands of children through its 'Free School Visits Scheme'. This 5-year programme from 2012-17 has offered outdoor learning sessions, from wetland exploration, to pond dipping, and bird & invertebrate identification.

~ MONITORING & PRIORITY SETTING ~

It's difficult to save wildlife if we don't know how many species exist and therefore which species we should be allocating most resources to in terms of conservation. The WWT's monitoring team regularly undertakes surveys to collect and assess the status of our waterbirds. This work brings together both governmental and non-governmental organisations; besides thousands of volunteers.

The Goose & Swan and the Seaduck Monitoring Programmes are two examples of initiatives that have ran since the early 1990s to improve the understanding of the current status of UK species. For example, early efforts were focused on the Common Scoter and its internationally important wintering site at Carmarthen Bay. Following the MV *Sea Empress* oil spill, the WWT undertook greater research to assess the oils disaster's impact on the main areas used by the Scoters. In turn, Carmarthen Bay was also recognised as the first marine Special Protection Area (SPA) in the UK.

~ SCALY-SIDED MERGANSER CONSERVATION ~

The Scaly-sided Merganser is part of the Mergus genus, which in the UK also includes the Smew, Goosander & Red-breasted Merganser.

It is one of the rarest seaducks of the Old World with a small population found in the remote Far East of Russia and China. The IUCN Red List classifies the specie as endangered with little information on its breeding status & ecology. Main losses have come from drowning in fishermen's gill nets during the birds' brood-rearing as well as from reduced nest-sites from tree logging in their riverine forest habitat.

The WWT has undertaken research & conservation work with Russian scientists in the principal Primorye breeding area. Artificial nest boxes (made from old car batteries) has been one of the great initiatives with over 1,000 ducklings hatched since the programme started some ten years ago. Geolocators have also been fitted to birds to monitor their migrations.

WETLANDS OF THE WORLD

EVERGLADES NATIONAL PARK
Located in Florida, USA, the Everglades is a vast, shallow and slow moving 'river of grass' that supports around 350 species of birds. It is one of only 3 landmarks to have the status of International Biosphere Reserve, World Heritage Site, and Wetland of International Importance.

OKAVANGO DELTA
This delta in Botswana is one of the world's most important inland waterways; hosting over 400 bird species. Given the scale and sheer splendour of the delta, its position in 2013 the position as one of the Seven Natural Wonders of Africa was secured.

TUNDRA FROZEN WETLANDS
Pools and bogs of the tundra are frozen for large parts of the year. During the summer, short thawing time yields vast numbers of insects & vegetative growth; important food sources for the birds. Many waterfowl in the northern hemisphere breed in this cold & treeless area around the Arctic Circle.

TAIGA BIOME
Extending across Europe, North America and Asia, the Taiga is the world's largest biome; 29% of forest coverage. It stores more freshwater & carbon than any other habitat. Tree nesting ducks as well as geese & swans travel to the taiga as food is plentiful & summer days lengthy.

KAKADU WETLANDS
In northern Australia, Kakadu is one of the planet's most valuable habitats for all kinds of wildlife. Four river systems feed into this floodplain, attracting a third of Australia's bird species. Kakadu is one of only a handful of places to hold Dual World Heritage Status.

THE PANTANAL
In South America, this is the largest freshwater wetland on Earth and a Natural Wonder of the World. The wet season means that 80% of the wetland is covered by water; eventually draining away in the dry season. Many waterfowl gather in the pools and channels formed.

KEEPING YOUR OWN WATERFOWL

In light of the many ways to occupy our time these days; the possibility of having a collection of ducks and geese in your own garden or piece of land is not always the obvious choice. However, not only does it provide a great way to enjoy more of the outdoors, but also much excitement as different events play out throughout the waterfowl's calendar year. It also does not require a great expanse of water or open field for them to roam. A small pond with a reasonable surround of plants and shrubs will satisfy a few pairs of ducks or geese or perhaps both!

~ CHECKLIST OF ESSENTIALS ~

Adequate fencing ~ Essential to stop your birds straying and protect them from predation by the likes of foxes, dogs, cats, stoats & polecats.

Permanent source of water ~ Should you want to keep ducks, then there must be a small amount of water at all times. Most ducks like to swim & bath; a man-made concrete pool or even an old tin bath sunk in the ground will do the trick. This should either be plumbed to keep the water fresh or manually changed as often as possible.

Plants, shrubs, reeds etc. ~ Make your enclosure a proper sanctuary. Plenty of greenery surrounding the water and the rest of the area will ensure your feathered friends can seek shelter, quiet time away from others, and of course somewhere to nest.

Do not overpopulate ~ Fitting as many birds in the space you have may look attractive, but this can cause aggravation between residents, limiting their breeding success and potentially leading to birds getting hurt for lack of escape.

Mixing the right species ~ There are so many different species of ducks and geese you may see, like and want to keep. The question of price and which birds will get along with each other and the home you provide is important to bear in mind. Get advice from other breeders first.

~ MANAGING THE COLLECTION ~

Ornamental vs. Domestic

The first question to ask yourself when starting your collection is whether you want ornamental (wild) waterfowl or their domesticated cousins; referred to as 'table ducks and geese'. A mixture of both is also possible if cared for correctly.

Although the domesticated varieties may not be as interesting in appearance or behaviour, they do have other characteristics that make them attractive choices. For a start, they are much cheaper to buy, are tamer and require less effort to rear. Besides this, they lay many more eggs that are fit for human consumption as well as the birds themselves... if that's your wish.

Feeding Regime

Catering for your collections' dietary needs is dependent on your choice of ornamental or domestic birds. The wild ornamental ducks & geese require a higher quality of food to maximise their health and wellbeing. This in turn will lead to a better chance of breeding, nesting and hatching success.

Most waterfowlers give two feeds per day; 1 morning and 1 afternoon or night. During breeding, a diet of purely breeder pellets (available from many feed merchants) should be fed. At the other times of year, this can be mixed half-half with wheat or mixed corn. Domestic ducks & geese can be given a similar pellet and corn mix for general poultry, consuming considerably more though.

The Breeding Season

Without doubt the most exciting time of year for the waterfowler, and busiest from a management aspect. Whether you have space to expand your collection or not, encouraging your birds to breed should always be an aim. There comes a time when you will have to replace members of your current collection, but up until that point surplus birds can be exchanged with other private collectors.

By following the checklist of essentials, i.e. not overpopulating, placing the right species together, and with plenty of places to nest, you should have some success. On the last point, nesting facilities may also take an artificial form, such as a box on the water's edge for dabbling ducks or on a tree for those that would use tree cavities when in the wild. Besides any shrubs planted, leaving piles of tree branches and uncultivated areas of grass will also provide simple & attractive nesting locations.

Hatching & Rearing

One of the older methods used to hatch and rear waterfowl is using a domestic duck or bantam. More often nowadays, most invest in an artificial incubating device when there are a greater number of eggs to hatch, but for just one or two pairs the original mothers can usually be trusted.

When rearing the offspring indoors – particularly for ducklings – a wooden box with a suspended infra-red heat lamp is the usual choice. Another popular arrangement is the semi-outdoor enclosure where more water is available to the young and the mother or foster parent is present. Other breeders will provide advice and designs of different rearing options and approaches during the time of acquiring your first birds.

Common Illnesses

Like all living creatures, waterfowl are no different in their susceptibility to illnesses & diseases. To maintain a healthy & thriving collection of waterfowl, it is important to be aware of these types of potential threats. Listed here are some of the more common illnesses & diseases that may be encountered.

Pneumonia ~ most common when a sudden change in the weather occurs. Exposure to cold and wet conditions may lead to pneumonia. Upon noticing signs of wheezing, coughing, choking or sneezing, you should visit the vet asap. Keeping the bird well wrapped up and in a warm place indoors is part of the treatment.

Angel wing ~ also referred to a slipped wing, this syndrome generally comes about when a bird has been fed a diet too high in protein in the early stages of its life. The bird will not suffer any pain with the condition, but the abnormal growth of the feathers pointing outwards does spoil their appearance.

Wet-feather ~ Birds suffering with this will either partially or fully lose the waterproofing in their feathers. Therefore, when they are exposed to the rain or attempting to swim, their feathers will absorb so much water to the extent they have no buoyancy and may even drown.

Coccidiosis ~ the droppings of the infected bird will show red blood and they will lose body weight as they cannot absorb the nutrients in food. Geese are more likely to pick the parasites from grazing on dirty ground where these occur. Not overstocking your enclosure will help to keep the ground as clean as possible.

Duck Virus Hepatitis ~ usually attacks ducklings in the first few weeks of life when their immune systems are still developing. Very quickly the disease can infect any of the ducklings reared together. Obvious signs are when a duckling's legs contract and they then die in an arched-back position.

~ ABOUT SOME DOMESTIC BREEDS ~

Muscovy duck
The only breed of utility duck that hasn't descended from the Mallard. The true wild form is mostly black; native to Mexico and Central & South America. The domestic birds are very broody, sitting 2-3 times/year.

Silver Appleyard duck
Created in the 1930s on the farm of Reginald Appleyard near Bury St. Edmonds, Suffolk. An all-round utility duck, laying up to 180 large white eggs each year; often going broody. Also regular foragers.

Indian Runner duck
Despite their name, these ducks are not from India but the Indonesian islands of Lombok, Java and Bali. Prolific egg layers that spend more time foraging than on water. They also cannot fly & occur in many colour variations.

Call duck
Their origins are uncertain; first thought to have been imported into Holland from Asia. Bred as decoys, given their talkative nature, used in large waterfowl traps to attract in the wild ducks. Mix easily with other breeds.

Aylesbury duck
Originated in Aylesbury, Buckinghamshire, in the early 18th century. Have always been popular for meat utility due to their size. The Pekin breed has become the preferred choice due to better egg & meat efficiency.

~ a few more DOMESTIC BREEDS...... ~

Buff Orpington duck
Created by William Cook of Orpington in Kent around 1890. They are thought to have been developed from the Aylesbury, Rouen, Cayuga and Indian Runner duck; giving them both good egg & meat production qualities.

Rouen duck
From the Rouen in France, these are a very old breed of domestic duck, bred for their table qualities. Their appearance resembles the wild Mallard, only darker. One of the heaviest domestic ducks, but slower growing.

Embden goose
One of the main breeds to be used for commercial meat production. Believed to have come from Emden in northern Germany, these geese are taller than most others but are often crossbred for a good utility bird.

Toulouse goose
Deriving from the countryside around Toulouse in Southern France. A very heavy goose developed to make pâté de foie gras. Placing birds in pairs will gain most breeding success, largely because males will often fight.

Pilgrim goose
Many believe these originated in England and were exported to other countries such as America. A tame and relatively quiet-natured goose that grows quickly. During breeding their behaviour can be more territorial.

~ A FEW RECOMMENDED WATERFOWL ~

When starting your collection of waterfowl there may be a temptation to pick those ducks and geese that have the more exotic appearances. However, as most breeders of waterfowl, including myself, would agree that ducks belonging to the dabbling duck tribe are the easiest and most manageable of the waterfowl to start off with.

These include Shoveler, Pintail, Teal, Wigeon & Gadwall that are wild UK residents. The majority of dabbling ducks are sociable and docile in nature, requiring shallower and less water compared to diving ducks. Many of the males and females also have distinct (dimorphic) plumages which helps to ensure you have a genuine pair of birds.

Here are some other non-UK resident species to consider upon start-up:

Fulvous Whistling-duck
The most widespread whistling-duck named for its rich cinnamon-buff feathers. They breed across the world's tropical regions, including Mexico & S. America. Shallow water with plentiful vegetation is the preferred habitat.

White-faced Whistling-duck
A highly sociable duck that in the wild breeds in sub-Saharan Africa and much of South America. The triple note 'whee-whee-whee' is sounded regularly as a contact call. Birds will nest in pairs or small colonies.

Falcated Teal
A medium-sized dabbling duck named after its black & white, sickle-shaped or falcated tertial feathers that extend over the rump. Generally silent with preference for water bodies providing plenty of cover.

Ringed Teal
A small duck that lives wild in forest habitats of South America. Unlike most ducks, they don't have an eclipse phase, therefore retaining their colourful plumage all year round. Pairs bond easily to breed.

Chestnut Teal
Found in southern Australia in the wild. They are small dabbling ducks that, unlike most others, form monogamous pairs beyond breeding. They prefer tree hollows; readily using artificial nest boxes.

Bahama Pintail
Females are very like males with a slightly less colourful orange-red on bill. They live in the Caribbean, S. America & Galapagos Islands. Quite a shy bird & usually kept in pairs or small groups.

Chiloé Wigeon
Its name comes from the Chiloé islands off the Chilean coasts. Like the European race, much time is spent grazing out of water. A very vocal duck, especially during courtship; pairs often form long term bonds.

Marbled Teal
Medium sized, feeding by diving and dabbling. Their restricted breeding range includes southern Spain, north-west Africa and western India & China. Gregarious and quiet; popular in captive collections.

MARVELS OF MIGRATION

There are many spectacular journeys undertaken by waterfowl that arrive en masse to the UK in winter. Here are a few examples.

The arctic tundra offers extensive day light hours for Bewick's to feed on the aquatic vegetation. Cygnets quickly gain the weight needed for migration in September.

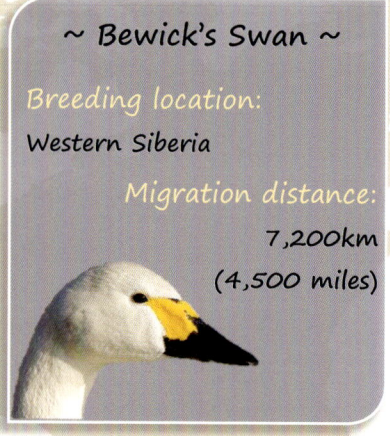

~ Bewick's Swan ~

Breeding location:
Western Siberia

Migration distance:
7,200km
(4,500 miles)

~ Eurasian Wigeon ~

Breeding locations:
Iceland, Russia, Norway, Sweden, Finland

Migration distance:
4,000km
(2,500 miles)

The Eurasian Wigeon is protected by the Agreement on the Conservation of African-Eurasian Migratory Waterbirds (AEWA). It focuses on birds that depend on wetlands for at least part of their lifecycle; crossing international borders during their migrations.

Breeding in eastern High Arctic Canada, the Light-bellied Brent stops via Greenland & western Iceland en route to their principal wintering grounds in Ireland, but also western Britain & further south in northern France.

~ Light-bellied Brent Goose ~

Breeding location:
Arctic Canada

Migration distance:
4,500km
(2,750 miles)

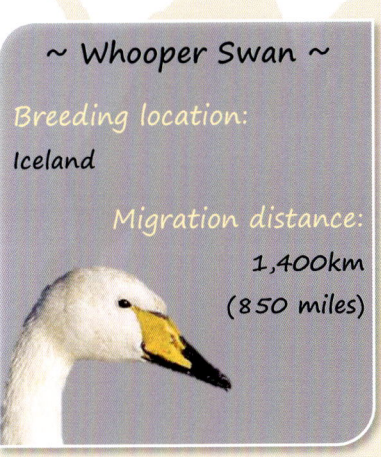

~ Whooper Swan ~

Breeding location:
Iceland

Migration distance:
1,400km
(850 miles)

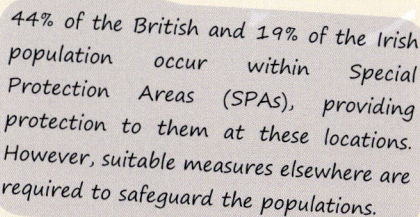

44% of the British and 19% of the Irish population occur within Special Protection Areas (SPAs), providing protection to them at these locations. However, suitable measures elsewhere are required to safeguard the populations.

*Migration distance is only one way.

MARVELS OF MIGRATION | 143

INDEX OF ENGLISH NAMES

B
Barnacle goose 28
Bean goose 31
Bewick's swan 14
Black swan 17
Brent goose 34

C
Canada goose 37
Carolina wood duck 54
Common Scoter 57

E
Eider 60
Egyptian goose 40

G
Gadwall 63
Garganey 66
Goldeneye 69
Goosander 72
Greylag 43

L
Long-tailed duck 75

M
Mallard 78
Mandarin 81
Mute swan 20

P
Pink-Footed goose 46
Pintail 84
Pochard 87

R
Red-breasted merganser ... 90
Ruddy duck 93

S
Scaup 96
Shelduck 99
Shoveler 102
Smew 105

T
Teal 108
Tufted duck 111

V
Velvet scoter 114

W
White-fronted goose 50
Whooper swan 23
Wigeon 117

INDEX OF LATIN NAMES

A

Aix galericulata 81
Aix sponsa 54
Alopochen aegyptiacus 40
Anas acuta 84
Anas clypeata 102
Anas crecca 108
Anas penelope 117
Anas platyrhynchos 78
Anas querquedula 66
Anas strepera 63
Anser albifrons 50
Anser anser 43
Anser brachyrhynchus 46
Anser fabalis 31
Aythya ferina 87
Aythya fuligula 111
Aythya marila 96

B

Branta bernicla hrota 13
Branta canadensis 37
Branta leucopsis 28
Bucephala clangula 69

C

Clangula hyemalis 75
Cygnus atratus 17
Cygnus columbianus 14
Cygnus cygnus 23
Cygnus olor 20

M

Melanitta fusca 41
Melanitta nigra 114
Mergus albellus 105
Mergus m. Merganser 72
Mergus serrator 90

O

Oxyura jamaicensis 93

S

Somateria mollissima 60

T

Tadorna tadorna 99

BIBLIOGRAPHY

A large part of the content of this book has been drawn from first-hand experience with my collection of waterfowl. In addition, inspiration has been taken from the work of other waterfowlers.

Here are some other great reads to further your understanding:

- BirdLife International (2017). *IUCN Red List for Birds.* [online] Available at: <http://www.birdlife.org> [Accessed 23 July 2017].

- Hume, R. (2013). *Complete Birds of Britain and Europe.* 4th edn. London: Dorling Kindersley Ltd.

- IUCN (2017). *The IUCN Red List of Threatened Species.* Version 2017-1. [online] Available at: <http://www.iucnredlist.org> [Accessed 22 July 2017].

- Johnson, A. A. & Payn, W. H. (1986). *Ornamental Waterfowl.* London: H. F. & G. Witherby Ltd.

- Ogilvie, M. & Young, S. (2002). *Wildfowl of the World.* London: New Holland Publishers Ltd.

- Ogilvie, M. (1982). *The Wildfowl of Britain and Europe.* New York: Oxford University Press.

- Scott, P. (2006). *Peter Scott's Coloured Key to the Wildfowl of the World.* The Wildfowl and Wetlands Trust.

- Soothill, E. & Whitehead, P.J. (1978). *Wildfowl of the World.* London: Peerage Books.

Quiz Answers

THE SWANS

 Questions on p.12

1. The Trumpeter swan, which is found in North America; males tip the scales at more than 15 kg and have a wingspan of over three metres.

2. Around 25,000. To put it into perspective, a bird of prey has between 5,000-8,000.

3. Once all the eggs have been laid, typically taking 2-3 weeks, they are incubated at the same time and will usually hatch up to 42 days (6 weeks) later.

4. The reason is that only the Monarch or a few specially favoured royal subjects could keep them and which they consumed as part of their grand banquets.

5. 'Swan Upping' is an annual census of the UK Mute swan population carried out on stretches of the River Thames. This event dates back to the 12th century, when the British Crown first claimed ownership of all unmarked Mute swans.

6. Swans of the northern hemisphere are almost entirely white in colour – the species are the Mute, Bewick's & Whooper. Those of the southern hemisphere are a mixture of white and black, comprising the Black Swan of Australia and the Black-necked Swan of South America.

THE GEESE

 Questions on p.26

1. The highest-flying goose in the world is the Bar-headed goose. They cruise at an altitude of 29,500 feet, higher than some commercial aircrafts. They have bigger wings than the average goose and a greater concentration of haemoglobin in the blood that carries the oxygen throughout their circulatory system.

2. The Canada goose, introduced to Britain in the 17th century, is the largest goose here with males weighing up to around 6 kg, 110 cm tall and with a wingspan of 1.7 metres. The Giant Canada goose from North America is the largest wild goose in the world, recorded with a weight of up to 9 kg.

3. The main reason is to conserve energy for their long migrations. Each bird in the flock flies slightly above the goose in front to reduce wind resistance. Each bird takes turn of leading at the front and the 'V' helps to keep track of each bird in the group; fighter aircraft pilots use this formation for the same reason.

4. The Brent goose has highly developed salt glands which enable it to consume saltier plant matter and water on the coastal marsh estuaries where it overwinters in Britain. The glands that excrete the excess salts are found in or on the skull area of the eye, nostril and mouth.

5. It is the Egyptian goose, native to sub-Saharan Africa. The first introductions in Britain were in the late 17th century for the collection of King Charles II in St James' Park, London. There are thought to be around 3,500 birds living here now.

6. The Light-bellied Brent goose travels around 5,500 miles each year between eastern High Arctic Canada and its wintering grounds in Ireland, western Britain & further south to northern France.

THE DUCKS

 Questions on p.52

1. The fastest recorded duck in flight is the Red-breasted Merganser, which is said to travel at speeds of around 100 mph. As a comparison, the Cheetah runs at speeds of up to 75 mph and the Peregrine falcon — the fastest member of the animal kingdom — around 240 mph.

2. The eclipse is the short period of time after breeding when the males of most species lose their brightly coloured plumage and thereby closely resembling the respective females. It is part of the annual cycle that allows them to regrow a fresh set of colourful feathers for the next breeding season.

3. All ducks are in fact omnivores, eating a combination of plants & animals. Plant matter includes grass, grains, fruit & berries and aquatic vegetation such as algae & pond weed, whilst the animals include molluscs (e.g. snails), worms, frogs, small fish and insects.

4. The most impressive diver of all the waterfowl is the Long-tailed duck. They can reach depths of up to 240 feet, yet there are instances when birds get caught in fishermen's nets, however.

5. Wigeon is our second most numerous duck spending time in the UK in the winter. Most of the world's Wigeon breed in Scandinavia and Russia with up to 500 pairs breeding in Britain, but around 450,000 journeying here from northern Europe and Asia come winter; this represents less than 20% of the world population.

6. It is false. Ducks are found on every continent except for the Antarctic. The closest inhabitant to the Antarctic is Eaton's Pintail, named after the naturalist & explorer Alfred Edmund Eaton. There are two subspecies, the Kerguelen & Crozet, named after the islands on which they live.